20/20

20 LEADERSHIP CONVICTIONS FOR THE WHOLE CHURCH IN 20 DAYS

Dr. Timothy C. Kernan, D. Min.

Printed in the United States of America and Europe

20/20: 20 Leadership Convictions For The Whole Church In 20 Days / Tim Kernan
ISBN-13: 978-1545091678
ISBN-10: 1545091676
First Print - First Edition

To my lovely wife Lianne and my sons TK and DK.

Note to Readers: Due to the advancements in printing technology, this book is printed as it is ordered. The printer allows us to upload a revised document at any time so that all subsequent books are corrected if an error is found. Please notify me of errors you notice and any comments or questions you have at tim@usd21.org as I will continue to edit the book.

Also, feel free to quote from this book and post hashtags in social media! This promotes the book and prayerfully encourages people as well!

It would be very much appreciated!

Contents

Acknowledgements 8

Introduction 11

Part 1: Impact 17

Conviction 1: Focus On The Few 18

Conviction 2: Wrestle For Miracles 35

Conviction 3: Sort Out The "Shenanigans" 47

Part 2: Fortify 72

Conviction 4: Get Them Leading Small Groups 74

Conviction 5: Bring To Unity 96

Conviction 6: Add Excellence 109

Part 3: Expand 118

Conviction 7: Fight From The Hills 119

Conviction 8: Fight The Road Battle 133

Conviction 9: Fry The Airwaves...145

Part 4: Exceed 153

Conviction 10: Build Conversion Power 154

Conviction 11: Be A Fish In The Water 166

Conviction 12: Preach The Word 177

Conviction 13: Worship God 190

Conviction 14: Serve To The Tears 200

Part 5: Overcome 211

Conviction 15: Love The Battle..212

Conviction 16: Advance The Gospel...................................... 226

Conviction 17: Join The Tribe.. 232

Conviction 18: Be Authentic 244

Conviction 19: Call To Decision 252

Conviction 20: Stay Strong In The Grace 268

Epilogue 277

Contact The Author:...279

Acknowledgements

First, all gratitude goes to God, who had an amazing plan for humanity, even though we did not merit it. God is the kindest, most merciful being in my life through Jesus Christ.

I would like to thank my wife Lianne for being an incredible partner in the Gospel, for working diligently by my side, and for giving me two awesome sons, Tim Jr. and David. After fourteen years of marriage, I hope that at last, I am learning how to be a good husband. Thank you, Lianne, for all your love and patience.

I also want to thank Kip and Elena McKean. I consider Kip the greatest theologian and ministry practitioner of our time. I appreciate his believing in me, his mentoring all these years, and for teaching me to depend on God and His Word, no matter what the circumstance or the consequence. I have never met another human being who preaches God's Word in every situation, as instinctively and powerfully as Kip, or who believes as strongly as Kip does that the Gospel is the solution to the world's problems. He is not merely trying to build a "great church" but he is laying down his life to take the heal a lost and broken world.

And as for his incredible wife, there is no woman I know with a more gentle and quiet spirit than Elena Garcia McKean. Many thanks to you both for your tireless devotion to God's Kingdom and His movement.

Much appreciation also goes to my brothers and sisters in the faith who befriended me, taught me, encouraged me and urged me forward over the past ten years: Kobi, who reached out to me and baptized me; Ghislain, who discipled me; Mr. Brown, who loves me; Danny, who gave me a shot; Andrew and Patrique, who pursue the ministry with all their hearts; Raul and Lynda, our dear friends; Kyle and Joan, true visionaries; Cory and Jee, new best of friends; Nick and Denise, family; Tony and Therese, fellow grill masters; Michael and Sharon, who care for so many; Michael and Michele, our "bro bro" and "sis sis"; Philippe and dear Prisca, for your hope in Christ; Thank you to Jason and Sarah, Blaise and Patricia, Ricky and Coleen, Ron and Tracy, Luke and Brandyn, LuJack and Cathi, Coltin and Mandy, Joel and Courtney, Mike and Brittany, Jared and Rachel, Kolbe and Rebecca, Nick and Jacque, and Ryan and Iyonna, for leading the Tribe and so many others that it would take another whole book to include!

Kip McKean preaching at the European Missions Conference in 2012.

Of very special note, I want to thank Dr. Kip McKean, Dr. Jen Watkins, Raul Moreno, Jason Dimitry, Chris Adams, LuJack Martinez, Evan Bartholomew, Jeanne McGee, Lisa Picciano Fellis, Heidi Santa Cruz and never least, my lovely wife Lianne, and my lovely mother Eleanor not only for your priceless editing help with this book but for always being there for me.

I have nothing except my God, His Kingdom and all of you.

PS: Special thank you to Starbucks and Buffalo Wild Wings for the early mornings and late nights of revisions!

Introduction

Welcome to **20/20: Twenty Biblical Leadership Convictions For The Whole Church In Twenty Days**, the first official edition. I initially wrote this book to record what I consider to be the most important ministry principles, and it later morphed into my ICCM Master's Thesis. For years, I have had those whom Lianne and I mentored and discipled read it so they could come to our times together prepared for a fruitful discussion. As a result, this book has had a life as a "guerrilla ministry" manual for some time. This edited and published version is light-years ahead of that PDF that is still circulating.

At the end of the day this book is my notes on the topic of visionary leadership for thirteen years of learning in Kip's Staff Meetings, leadership classes and formal Bible school. If anything that is written here is a misunderstanding of the Bible then "eat the fish and spit out the bones." On the other hand, if it helps even two young people to choose to be leaders in God's Kingdom and love the Bible more, then I am satisfied. I am not suggesting that I am an expert at accomplishing all about which I am writing. Like you I am continuing to learn from the Scriptures. As well, many of the practicals of this book come from my own trial and error, certainly not perfection.

My goal with this book is to share with you twenty indispensable leadership convictions that everyone in God's church can learn and use. Perhaps you will read it and discuss it with those with whom you are striving in the ministry. Often, the only difference between a surviving group and a thriving group of disciples is the presence of leaders who are motivated to lead according to the principles of the Bible - that is what this book is all about.

Why do I say that leadership is for the whole church? Jesus was a leader; therefore everyone in the church who wants to be like Jesus will want to be a leader.

Why twenty convictions or principles? The number forty has significance in the Bible as the number representing sanctification or readiness. Note the following examples: the world was flooded for forty days to purify it; manna fell for forty years; the people of Israel wandered for forty years before they were ready to enter the promised land; the spies surveyed the land for forty days; the maximum punishment was forty lashes; Jesus prayed and fasted for forty days before He began His powerful ministry; Jesus taught the Apostles about the Kingdom for forty days, etc. It is the number of maturity and preparedness.

In a similar way the number twenty, or half of forty, is the number of qualification or beginning. In Genesis 31:38, Jacob worked for Laban for twenty years before he could begin his household. In Genesis 37:28, Joseph began his journey to Egypt when his brothers sold him for twenty shekels of silver. In Exodus 30:14, all those twenty years of age or older were accountable for an offering to the Lord. In Numbers 1:3, the Bible commands all able-bodied men over the age of twenty to serve in the army. In Numbers 14:29, God punished everyone who was twenty years of age or more who had grumbled against Him. In 1 Kings 6:20, *"The inner sanctuary was twenty cubits long, twenty wide and twenty high. [Solomon] overlaid the inside with pure gold, and he also overlaid the altar of cedar."* In 1 Kings 9:10, it took twenty years to build the first temple and the royal palace. In Ezra 3:8, Levites twenty years of age and older could *"...supervise the building of the house of the Lord."* There are twenty chapters in this book because this represents the beginning of the road to understanding Jesus' visionary leadership principles of ministry, not the end.

As I mentioned before, this book has had a life of its own for some time, as a sort of unofficial training manual for my ministry. I have revised and rewritten it a "zillion" times based on discussions with many leaders and friends. It has come together from over 250 sermons, church bulletins and articles that I have written over the years.

"For since the creation of the world God's invisible qualities - His eternal power and divine nature - have been clearly seen, being understood from what has been made, so that people are without excuse." (Romans 1:20) God's principles can be learned through everyday work and even sports. As a Brazilian Jiu-jitsu fighter, I was always impressed by the superiority of technique over strength. It is amazing to see small fighters skillfully defeat much larger opponents using method over brute force. This is a very Christian principle, and through Jiu-jitsu God has taught me to depend on the Spirit and Jesus' teaching rather than on my power. In ministry, we will face many problems that cannot be overcome with our intelligence, talent, and strength. I also was impressed at how Jiu-jitsu fighters, like people in most sports, collect, practice and perfect "moves" such as the famous "armbar," "scissor sweep," "hip escape," etc. I realized that in ministry we really did not have a similar collective vocabulary and set of key techniques.

In some ways, this influenced how I wrote 20/20 because I wanted to provide a "shared terminology" that will help leaders utilize Jesus' effective and God dependent techniques. I hope that chapters such as "Join The Tribe," "Fight From The Hills," "Love The Battle," etc., will become terms that will help you be victorious in your everyday life and ministry challenges.

I actually started with only five or six chapters. They were like buckets, in a sense, and I tried to fit everything I had learned into them. However, many of the principles simply did not fit into my original chapters and really needed to become their own chapters. Overtime this book grew from a handful to twenty chapters. My prayer is that you as the reader will seek the ways of Jesus' ministry and find many more principles that you can share with others in turn.

As I edit this book for publication, I cannot help but consider the looming backdrop of the desperate needs of God's church today. She cries out for prepared, reliable men and women to lead the charge in evangelizing this hostile and anti-Christian world. As disciples of Jesus Christ we are all called to be *"strong in the grace"* (1 Timothy 2:1) and to establish flourishing Christian groups where now there are none. Indeed, contrary to the rosy picture painted by false preachers and ideologues, billions of people are slaves to the lies told by *"Satan who leads the whole world astray."* (Revelation 12:9)

In 2 Corinthians 10:3-5, the Bible states:

> *For though we live in the world, we do not wage war as the world does. The weapons we fight with are not the weapons of the world. On the contrary, they have divine power to demolish strongholds. We demolish arguments and every pretension that sets itself up against the knowledge of God, and we take captive every thought to make it obedient to Christ.*

If humbly understood and applied, the Scriptures possess a power from God to demolish the oppressive strongholds that imprison our families, neighbors, communities, and nations in painful toil. As leaders (and once again, every Christian is called to lead), we believe that the Scriptures contain principles and strategies upon which we can build deep convictions.

What is a "strategy?" It is simply "a plan of action... designed to achieve a major or overall aim." What is a "conviction?" The word conviction comes from the Latin word "convictio" which means "to have seen it proven." That is why we search the Scriptures day and night to learn the "proven" direction in which we must take our ministries. The convictions that we can build from the Scriptures have the power to free all people and to usher them into God's Kingdom. My prayer is that this book will help you accomplish just that. In the next twenty days, we will cover twenty essential Bible convictions both to advance our ministries and to avoid ultimate defeat.

It has often been observed that people enter the ministry with one conviction, strategy, or plan to attain their goal - optimism. However, within even a short period, optimism by itself will not be enough to overcome the obstacles of the ministry. If people who have optimism as their plan suffer enough defeats, they will develop a new coping strategy in their ministry - pessimism. Far too many "would-be ministers" have only optimism in their toolbox and eventually - because of the imminent pessimism to follow - leave their calling. They sit on the sidelines of the church and watch cynically as others take the field.

Instead of going back and forth between optimism and pessimism, why not build Biblical convictions in our ministry work and watch God's ways bring God's results? Why not learn Jesus' ministry - the way Jesus led? We need to constantly be learning and building deeper convictions about Jesus' Scriptural methods and visionary Scriptural leadership. Each Biblical lesson gives us another card to play if we do not give up. *"Let us not become weary in doing good, for at the proper time we will reap a harvest if we do not give up. Therefore, as we have the opportunity, let us do good to all people, especially to those who belong to the family of believers."* (Galatians 6: 9-10)

I am so blessed to have studied with many incredible ministers who led according to the principles of the Bible. Practicing brilliant Biblical strategies and ideologies, these men have taught me invaluable lessons and have deepened my convictions about how to build an effective and thriving Christian ministry. Through their expert handling of the Scriptures, these practitioners - whom I will be quoting in this book - have helped me to build clear, attainable convictions on what were once murky subjects. The goal of this book is to share these essential leadership convictions with all of Christ's disciples - God's leaders.

Another prayer is that this book will inject all of us with twenty inspiring "eureka" moments of Jesus' leadership. In twenty days, anyone can totally change the way he or she sees the ministry. They can learn the Biblical way to transform that ministry to become a work that brings glory to God and encouragement to His people.

Finally, it is also my prayer that Christian leaders who are more astute than me will be encouraged by this book to write, teach and preach about strategies, principles and ministry lessons that they have acquired over their years of ministry practice. In reality, there are few books on the actual practice of ministry. My heartfelt prayer is that this book will be one of the first among many that deal with the practice of Christian ministry as true disciples of Jesus Christ - a topic that has inspired me since the first moment I learned about it. Let us now explore the treasures and exotic lands of knowledge that are the Bible! Let us get into our study of Biblical ministry principles and face the future with the clarity of 20/20 vision!

Tim Kernan

★

The following three convictions are the results of my first conversation that I had with Kip McKean when I asked for his counsel about a ministry I was leading at the time. On that cloudy August morning in 2004, at the Starbucks across the street from the Ambridge Event Center in Portland, Oregon, I began to build convictions that have become key for me in the subsequent years of my ministry.

Kip compressed decades of Biblical experience into three pieces of advice:

1. "Focus on the few and impact their lives. If you focus on everyone, you focus on no one."
2. "Show the miracles. God's Word is always fruitful."
3. "Build a base of sold-out disciples."

That talk changed my life and ministry forever. His advice was Biblical, practical and insightful. I asked myself the following questions: Had I focused on the incredible disciples who were close to me and wanted to be raised up? Had I truly relied on God and His Word? Were there miracles occurring in my ministry? Had I avoided conflicts with people who needed to be won over to true discipleship? These were the questions I had to answer. The answers would help me as well as those that God put in my life to develop the convictions necessary to build a flourishing ministry.

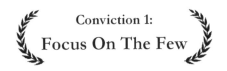

Conviction 1:
Focus On The Few

"If you focus on everyone, you focus on no one. By focusing on the few, you significantly impact their lives, and they in turn impact the lives of many others." Kip McKean

Jason and Sarah Dimitry are the dynamic leaders of the San Francisco International Christian Church.

You then, my son, be strong in the grace that is in Christ Jesus. And the things you have heard me say in the presence of many witnesses entrust to reliable people who will also be qualified to teach others. (2 Timothy 2:1-2)

> *"If you focus on everyone, you focus on no one."*

Disciples training disciples; this is the method Jesus used to reach an entire lost world that was starving for His mercy. What Jesus did was to start by gathering a few disciples who in turn would be leaders, and leaders of leaders. In other words, Jesus invested Himself fully in a comparatively small number of disciples, whom He called to imitate His life and ministry.

"One of those days Jesus went out to a mountainside to pray, and spent the night praying to God. When morning came, He called His disciples to Him and chose twelve of them, whom He also designated Apostles..." (Luke 6:12-13) In calling out the Twelve, Jesus chose the men in whom He wanted to invest. This was not a choice Jesus made lightly. It was so important to choose the right people that He prayed about it all night. This selection of followers for "discipling" (for lack of a better word to describe the practice of disciple-making) resulted in twelve powerful Apostles who changed the world in their generation.

In 2 Timothy 2:1-2, Paul encouraged Timothy to imitate the same model as Jesus and the Apostles. By devoting himself to a small group of committed disciples, Timothy could build a circle of leaders who would be able to impact others. Paradoxically, by focusing himself and investing in fewer people, his impact would become even more powerful and extensive. This Biblical truth, counterintuitive as it may seem, needs to become second nature to us as well.

For me, this principle was never made clearer than when my lovely wife and I were sent by the Holy Spirit from London to Los Angeles in 2010 to lead the South Region of the mighty City of Angels International Christian Church (CAICC). The South Region was a small group in Long Beach - only 19 disciples to start - and yet I knew that caring for every need of even 19 disciples, not to mention growing the group, would be exhausting for Lianne and I alone. So we set about building a small, focused group of promising leaders who would be the future Bible Talk Leaders of the ministry.

Tim and Lianne Kernan, Jason and Sarah Dimitry, Raul and Lynda Moreno spy out the land for the Rio De Janeiro (Brazil) planting.

Soon, we both had a chosen "few" with whom we were working. Of all the awesome disciples who rose up, the one who became a best friend and close confidante to me was my brother Jason Dimitry. Jason was a talented disciple with an amazing, down-to-earth, practical and streetwise mindset. He had a somewhat checkered past;

yet God worked it out that Jason would be truly and fully committed to Him by the time of my arrival in LA. It became quite clear in a short amount of time that he would be "my Timothy." (2 Timothy 2:2) Having a close best friend and right-hand man or woman is a very important part of focusing on the few. As with Jesus and Paul, we must focus on the few, but even within those few, we give that extra little bit to just one.

Jason and I not only became the best of friends, but Jason soaked up everything I could teach him about the Bible and the ministry. Every day we spent time together evangelizing, studying our Bibles, and dreaming of what God would do with our South Region Ministry. He wanted to be in the ministry so badly, but as a thirty-something divorcee with two kids, he felt that the full-time ministry was out of reach. This was something that saddened him quite a lot.

In our time together, we saw the addition of nearly 60 committed disciples and the sending out of two mission teams from our ministry. Truth be told, I learned as much from Jason as he learned from me. The miracles that happened because of our friendship and discipling relationship was a true blessing from God. Jason's humility and hard work made him shine like a star in the eyes of the brothers and sisters; especially one sister in the London Church - Sarah Travis! It was not long before Jason was an "unpaid intern" for the church. His humility had paid off in an incredible way. Sarah became Jason's sweetheart, and I had the honor of serving as Jason's best man on August 13, 2011. Together, along with their four children, they now make up the happy Dimitry family.

The Dimitrys planted the mighty Las Vegas International Christian Church and currently lead the powerful San Francisco International Christian Church. I believe that there are no limits as to what God can do with Jason. I continue to pray for him every day, even as I write this chapter from Chennai, India, on the Bay of Bengal. Jason's example additionally illustrates for us that it is not just our focus on the few - it is also the humility of the chosen to be part of someone else's few. Without the humility to follow "a man," we will never lead "other men" effectively.

There is so much to think about regarding "focus on the few." First off, how many are "a few?" For some, a few might be two or three; for others, it might be 10 or more. A few is the number that allows us to have a dramatic impact in the life of each person. One way to think about "focusing on the few" is just to build a group of best friends. It is in small groups like this that we find our "Joshuas" (Moses' successor), "Jonathans" (David's closest friend), and "Peters" (Jesus' right-hand man).

A practical side note to keep in mind: it is hard to focus on a few when those few we have chosen have secular jobs. Jesus put His guys on "full-time" as quickly as he could. Often, creative solutions were required (Luke 8:3)!

"Tone" is so important in ministry. How we say or do something is always as important as what we say and do. In setting the tone for discipling relationships, coaching is often the best model to follow. Too often discipling relationships are not coaching relationships, aimed at attaining goals, but more like parole officer-parolee relationships, aimed at preventing relapses! Again, how we focus on the few can be as important as the *"careful instruction"* (2 Timothy 4:2) we give. We must pull in our few like Jesus pulled in the Apostles, or like a black belt pulls in his martial arts students, with competence and confidence, preparing them for greatness - not just to prevent failure. We must give to each of our few as their specific needs require.

On the other hand, "the few" must have appropriate expectations for the discipling they will receive. *"Like apples of gold in settings*

of silver is a word spoken in right circumstances. (Proverbs 25:11 NASB) When we receiving fitting and accurate discipling we should be overjoyed! That being said, some expect a truck load of diamonds every discipleship time while others are prepared to accept a dump truck full of rocks with some diamonds in it. Good quality discipling that has "truth to it" should be good enough. If we become too picky we will miss out on many good diamonds of discipling.

The opposite of focusing on "the few" is focusing on "the many." The many is any number that weakens our impact. Far too many passionate, well-intentioned ministers have burned out because they spread themselves too thin. "A focus on everyone is a focus on no one." Also, burn-out is a terrible, albeit predictable, consequence of not following Jesus' example of multiplication through investing in the few. There is no substitute for God's plan of discipleship to accomplish His eternal purposes.

What stops so many people from becoming good disciplers of a "few?" The truth of the matter is that discipling is the scariest thing in the world. It is the "Mirror of Truth" into which all who claim to have faith must look. The danger of rejection, loss of investment, abuse of power, and hurt is so great that many "strong Christians" have run from it in terror. Discipling requires true vulnerability, faith and confidence in God that few people choose to have.

A leader who focuses on the few must be wise, faithful and confident enough in God to be the most vulnerable first. He must be the one to give trust first, as well as to confess his most embarrassing sins first. This creates an atmosphere of understanding, compassion, trust and openness between fully committed disciples of Jesus Christ. Once this atmosphere of trust is established between two men or women of God, the foundation for effect tive training in ministry is set.

"Focus" does not mean there will be no more "bumps" or problems. In fact, there may be more. However, in discipling relationships, "problems" are not problems; as my discipler says, "Problems are discipling opportunities!" Jesus saw the sparks that fly in discipling relationships and the circumstances of life as the perfect way to train and strengthen His disciples. *"As iron sharpens iron, so one person sharpens another."* (Proverbs 27:17)

We maximize our training of the few by forming them into a group. By working together in group settings, be it a social occasion or a formal discipling group, we are provided with powerful opportunities for camaraderie, fellowship and training. In a discipleship group settings, the leader gathers with his few for worship, prayer, confession and deeper Biblical study, and from time to time - fun. The discipleship group is a team where the leader provides "discipling" - Scriptural direction and practical guidance.

The leader of this team must be discerning, aiding "his" disciples in building great relationships with each other. This allows them to disciple one another. The leader must always make sure that the truth is spoken in love, even though that love may sometimes hurt. He must also anticipate the sins that will inevitably surface in this group setting: jealousy, insecurity, anger, selfish ambition, etc. Imitating Jesus, the leader must be prepared to use these "golden discipling opportunities" to foster growth and maturity. Discipling groups are an indispensable tool of focusing on the few.

Lianne and I - now leading the City of Angels International Christian Church of 1,000 disciples as well as the Western USA, Canada and Haitian Churches - have continued our quest to focus on "the few." Our "few" today are the Overseeing Evangelists and Women's Ministry Leaders, Administrators and City of Angels Church Shepherds. This potentially could create a separation between

Lianne and I from the high potential, young ministry people in the City of Angels Church. However, Jesus ministry provides an example here as well. Jesus not only had a 12, but He also played a role in the 70 which was the "few" of His "few." (Luke 10:1) We do this today through our "Armor-Bearers" and "Shield Maidens" Fraternity and Sorority. These brothers and sisters are the right-hand men and women, the reliable "few," for our Region Leaders. By pulling these young men and women together into a "group of 70" setting, we can invest in them and in turn help our few to raise up their powerful few.

The author gathered his valiant "Armor Bearers Fellowship" on October 8, 2016.

Part of the art of working with a few is knowing when to gather them in (Mark 6:30) and when to send them out. (Matthew 10:5) "Focus" does not necessarily mean constantly looking over the shoulder of our disciples. In the paraphrased words of a famous coach named Mike Krzyzewski, "You need to know when to give them a play and when to let them play." It takes practice to get this right.

Likewise, teach the older women to be reverent in the way they live, not to be slanderers or addicted to much wine, but to teach what is good. Then they can urge the younger women to love their husbands and children, to be self-controlled and pure, to be busy at home, to be kind, and to be subject to their husbands, so that no one will malign the Word of God.
(Titus 2:3-5)

Lianne Kernan with her lovely and talented "Shield Maidens" at their Spring Fling on May 7, 2017.

Simultaneously, as the ministry leader is focused on his few, he must also disciple a mature sister - usually his wife, but not always - who will disciple her "few" sisters. It is critical that the women's ministry is run by the same "focus on the few" strategy as the men's ministry. In particular, with married disciples, husbands must disciple their wives as implied in the Scripture above. However, wives also need a spiritually mature female mentor who can help as well. In other words, a husband must wash his wife with the Word (Ephesians

26

5:26), but according to Scripture, there must also be a women's discipling network (Titus 2:3-5) to support the wives.

The young women who have become daughters in the faith to Lianne and I by aiding us so much in our ministry: Heidi and Devon, (bottom left to right) Jessie, Tajai and Xanthe (top left to right).

In the women's ministry, one of the "few" for a sister with children, should be her "nanny." The world teaches that a woman should be able to have three kids, a husband, a job, do it all on her own, and look like a magazine model. This is why it is said that one in four women in the western world is on mental health medication for conditions such as depression and anxiety.[1] Sisters with children often do not feel entitled to receive help from younger sisters, because they did not help anyone with their children. Therefore, they feel hypocritical when they ask for help.

---

[1] *Women And Prescription Drugs: One In Four Takes Mental Health Meds:* The Huffington Post November 16, 2011.

Often they are also afraid to seek help from peers for many reasons, which really boils down to pride. Moreover, many of these same women have not fostered any mentoring relationships with older more experienced sisters. (Titus 2:3-5) Frequently, the only person they feel comfortable delegating to is their husband. As a result, instead of one overwhelmed person, now there are two. The whole family is taken out. They then come to the "realization" that they cannot serve in ministry and need to back off the church and ultimately, God. Meanwhile, a single sister is watching five hours of Netflix a few blocks over and struggling because her ex non-Christian boyfriend is texting her again.

A sister with children might not have much money to offer, but she does have food and companionship, the ability to help her nanny get dates with spiritual brothers, and be an overall big sister. In nature, this is called a symbiotic relationship that is very beneficial to both parties! A leadership sister with kids, who has not built a great relationship with several younger sisters who can help her, is in for an unnecessarily hard life. On the other hand, a sister who does make her nanny one of her "few" not only raises up another leader but thoroughly enjoys the ministry.

Focusing on the few is not about teaching behaviors, but about transferring heart and exemplifying lifestyle: person to person, brother to brother, sister to sister. Heart and lifestyle stay with people, even when everything else "melts away." That means observing those you disciple carefully by spending considerable time with them, thus creating memories, showing them the rewarding lifestyle of Christianity. I love Jason Dimitry's saying, "Imitation is suicide." True imitation requires dying to oneself and imitating Jesus by those who Jesus has put in our lives! (1 Thessalonians 1:6)

Some might say, "Wow, discipling a few sounds like hard work. I just do not have that kind of time with all my responsibilities. My plate is full enough as it is with all my duties!" It is true that having an impact on the lives of other disciples does take a lot of energy and focus. However, in practice, within a short period the "few" will become very competent and excellent helpers. This means that we can start to delegate duties to them and work through them, multiplying our energy, and impacting the world. This also gives you more time to evangelize, have more Bible studies with non-Christians, and be more effective overall!

The City of Angels International Christian Church Super Region Leader Couples: The Rohns, Feumbas, Hardings, Kernans, Underhills and Challinors.

Moreover, consider this Scripture: *"He is the one we proclaim, admonishing and teaching everyone with all wisdom, so that we may present everyone fully mature in Christ. To this end I strenuously contend with all the energy Christ so powerfully works in me."* (Colossians 1:28-29) It is not about us it is about proclaiming Christ. We must admonish and teach, but Jesus is going to give us his energy as we go! We cannot give up on our people before we even start.

After walking side-by-side for a time with our few, we can begin to disciple them through supervision and oversight rather than hands-on, daily working together. That being said, before we get too comfortable delegating, remember to "inspect what you expect." We should never "delegate and disappear," because then we forfeit the ability to perfect our few. We then fall into the trap of assuming they are ready to do what we do, with the heart and faith with which we do it. Timothy still needed Paul to disciple him even after he was leading a church - our few still need us even as they mature and grow to do even greater things in their ministries. We are never done focusing on a few.

The Speckmans have done an incredible job raising up the McDonnells!

Some might say that focusing on a few neglects the weak. In fact, the contrary is true. When you focus on the few and strengthen them they then multiply the number of leaders who can meet the needs of the weak. Therefore, anyone who truly have a passion for the weak will focus on "the few."

What is key - and many successful ministry people do this daily - is to update their list of the most vulnerable, weak disciples. They often keep the list on their phone and use their few, such as their shepherding couples, to go after helping these precious souls. When we keep that list short, by helping the vulnerable to get spiritually strong, our whole ministry is stronger. We cannot focus on everyone, but we are responsible for making sure that everyone's needs are met through our leaders and shepherds.

In campus ministry, on average, we have about three years before our members graduate and head out into other ministries. That is not a bad thing because the campus ministry provides many young faithful leaders for other ministries. The downside is that our whole ministry will disappear before our eyes in a very short period if we are not growing it powerfully. As a church leader, it is essential that some of our "few" come from our campus ministry, or that our "few" have disciples that are in the campus ministry.

If we neglect our campus ministry for a few years, it will "graduate out." The consequence of this is that the average age of our membership will skyrocket and the church will eventually atrophy and die. As such, it is critical for us to either be on campus ourselves or to have our most capable "few" on campus daily to grow this essential ministry.

When Lianne and I first came to the City of Angels International Christian Church and led the South Region, we discipled as our few many campus students at Long Beach State, Cerritos College and Long Beach Community College. Today, eight years later, we do not disciple any campus students; however we ensure that our few are discipling campus students and are on the campus every day forcefully advancing this incredible ministry!

Looking at "focus on the few" from another perspective, it is also important to be a part of someone else's "few." Leaders who do not have excellent discipling relationships themselves feel insecure and lack the direction necessary to be truly effective. Their decision-making can become incredibly weak due to a lack of input and Scriptural advice. They flounder and quite often their situation can become very negative before they "humble out" and see their need to be discipled. Experience has shown time and time again that the most powerful leaders allow themselves to get "adopted" by exemplary "fathers in the faith" whom they wish to imitate. As our dear sister, Rebecca Rico said as she boarded the plane for London, England, "I am going to get myself adopted by Michael and Michele Williamson!" (Michael and Michele are the powerful church leaders of London.)

The true leader in the Kingdom of God is a master discipler. Like a "Jedi Knight" of the Star Wars Films they raise up "padawan learners" who become Jedi themselves. The opposite of a master discipler is a "demagogue." The term demagogue comes from the Greek word *dēmos* meaning "people" and *agōgos* meaning "leading." While not negative on its own, this term has been used since ancient times for rabble-rousers, agitators and provocateurs. Absalom was an example of a demagogue. (2 Samuel 15-18) A demagogue seeks tribute, not discipling. While enjoying financial gain and perhaps even sporting an entourage, the Bible does not recognize the televangelist or put him on the same footing as a true preacher and discipler described in the Scriptures.

Jealousy and selfish ambition may rear its ugly head when appointing your few. This should not deter us but rather we should see this as a a "discipling opportunity." ***"You are still worldly. For since there is jealousy and quarreling among you, are you not worldly? Are you not acting like mere humans?"*** (1 Corinthians 3:3) One does not find out how God feels about them from the role they have in the church. They learn that from looking upon the cross. We must teach our membership that raising up leaders is simply what we do in the church. Moreover, the workload with which we will saddle "the few" will ease any feeling that we are giving "privileges" rather than godly duty and responsibility.

Although discipling is the plan of Jesus, let us not get too excited. We are warned in Proverbs 21:30, *"There is no wisdom, no insight, no plan that can succeed against the Lord,"* and again in verse 31, *"The horse is made ready for the day of battle, but victory rests with the Lord."* Can we confidently advance with our firm grasp of proper discipling and our many "war horses" and have victory without a great relationship with God? The answer is a resounding and definitive "no." Discipling is how God wants to evangelize the world, but the victory itself rests with the Lord - always. This is a frightening calculation: Discipling minus daily walk with God equals defeat. Let us never take our minds off of this important truth.

On the other hand, Jesus' plan of discipling is a powerful and essential strategy to evangelize the world in our generation. Is it a substitute for prayer? Absolutely not! By the same token, prayer is no substitute for obedience to God's plan either!

In our younger years of ministry, when we have fully built and trained our "few," then comes the victory! Victory is giving them away and sending them out! What? Yes! After investing in someone for a period, that person might then be called on to go out into the mission field or to go help support another ministry. It is very important to make them understand that this is a victory and not a "defeat." As we focus on our few, we need to be sure we are always conveying the message that the objective of our discipling is to prepare them for the moment they are chosen by God to carry out His mission and go where they are needed.

We need to aim to make our ministry an exporter of leaders and missionaries, with our discipleship group serving as the primary "port of departure." We do not want our ministry to become a place where Christians stagnate and become "dead-end disciples," or worse, a net importer of leadership, which hurts the rest of the church.

All this being said, as we age our few become a solidified group which indeed we can send in and out. Most likely though as with Timothy and Paul, our discipling relationships become lifelong partnerships. I am now 41 years old and I thoroughly enjoy my discipling relationship with Kip. As a matter of fact we probably talk two to four times every day! As well now Lianne and I are in the process of selecting our lifelong few such as Jason and Sarah Dimitry, Ricky and Coleen Challinor, among others.

Focusing on the few is difficult to start. There will be many times when we will have to "get back up on the horse." However, it will become easier as our few mature and become better partners in the Gospel to us. Focusing on the few is about pulling them in to "give them the play," but then knowing when to "let them play." It is about tenderly healing and strengthening the weak like a loving and nurturing mother and father. (1 Thessalonians 1-2) It is about advancing positively and working with those willing to do great things for God. It is about raising up new leaders from the campus and teen ministries. At the end of the day, focusing on the few is about being like Jesus, obeying His teachings, and learning more and more about how awesome He is. Focusing on the few is about freeing a lost world that so desperately needs revolutionaries to take up its cause in the name of the Lord!

Conviction 2:
Wrestle For Miracles

When you as God's man or woman show up on the scene, decisive miracles happen quickly. Show the miracles of God that "accredit" you and advance the ministry dramatically. (Acts 2:22)

**The amazing baptism of Alexis Turgeau -
Father of Faith for Haiti!**

The most powerful miracle worker of all time was Jesus. *"During the days of Jesus' life on earth, He offered up prayers and petitions with fervent cries and tears to the one who could save Him from death, and He was heard because of His reverent submission."* (Hebrews 5:7) No one ever fought, wrestled and sacrificed for miracles like Jesus. Incredibly He says this of us, *"Very truly I tell you, whoever believes in me will do the works I have been doing, and they will do even greater things than these, because I am going to the Father."* (John 14:12)

"Whoever" believes in Jesus will do the works he was doing; in fact, they will do *"even greater things!"* This Scripture should encourage every disciple and leader! It means that Jesus expects anyone who believes in Him to have an even greater impact than He did while He was on the earth! This is amazing! It means that the ministry of a man or woman of God is not dull or mediocre, but rather exploding with powerful miracles! Be it on campus or in a regular church setting - no matter how bad the situation is - when God's man or woman appears, things start to happen, and happen quickly. Not at all because he or she is awesome... but because his or her God is!

As we think about being miracle workers, let us reflect on the dramatic Scripture below. When Jacob sent all his wives, children and belongings ahead of him toward his estranged brother Esau, he knew he would need a miracle from God. When they all went ahead of him,

> *...Jacob was left alone, and a man wrestled with him till daybreak. When the man saw that he could not overpower him, he touched the socket of Jacob's hip so that his hip was wrenched as he wrestled with the man. Then the man said, "Let me go, for it is daybreak." But*

Jacob replied, "I will not let you go unless you bless me."

The man asked him, "What is your name?" "Jacob," he answered. Then the man said, "Your name will no longer be Jacob, but Israel, because you have struggled with God and with man and have overcome." Jacob said, "Please tell me your name." But he replied, "Why do you ask my name?" Then he blessed Him there. (Genesis 32:22-29)

Here, Jacob, whose name means "the deceiver," receives his new and famous name "Israel," which means "wrestles with God." Jacob wrestles for the blessing that he wants and receives it after persevering in a grueling wrestling match with "a man," possibly the pre-incarnate Christ, that lasted until daybreak. Most people just give up when the first answer is "no," but this was not Israel's way! That night, he must have bitten the dust time and time again, yet he continued fighting until he received what he so desperately desired. Israel's tenacity and boldness always amaze me!

Today, nothing has changed! Just as in the time of Israel, it is God who grants the blessings and God who grants the miracles. *"Don't be deceived, my dear brothers and sisters. Every good and perfect gift is from above, coming down from the Father..."* (James 1:16-17) Without God's blessings nothing good will happen in our ministries.

I will never forget flying into London, England, in the fall of 2007 to lead a small group of four amazing Christians who represented our church in London. I was immediately a little awestruck by England and its grandeur. As an Irish-Canadian with Irish Republican heritage, I was happy to leave old divisions behind and lead God's people in England. I remember getting off the plane at

Gatwick Airport and feeling so humbled with this responsibility. Meeting me at the airport were the "faithful few" disciples: Oliver and Eugenie Greenwood, Jason Green and Stephen Fraser. None of us were terribly experienced, and yet we had faith, and we were ready to wrestle with God to see great things happen!

That very night we set to work dreaming and scheming for God to move with our small group. We prayed, fasted, agreed, dreamed, risked everything, decided to love one another - and God's heart was moved.

**Oliver Greenwood was the brother with the dream for a
church of sold-out disciples in London!**

Over the course of the next two-and-a-half years, so many incredible miracles happened that we cannot list them all here. Indeed, our experience in London became a formative time for Lianne and I in our ministry journey. We saw so many people join our little group of disciples through baptism and restoration. Of note, some amazing disciples placed membership from the ICOC. Among them were Jacques and Jeanette Groenewald from South Africa, with whom we became best friends; Ola Kukoi of Nigeria; Megan Bard (now Studer) from Canada; James and Deirdre Morgan from Ireland; and about two dozen others.

The disciples sacrificed so deeply that we went from being a church with a monthly income of about £120[2] ($240 US) to £67,000 ($134,000 US)[3] per year with a full-time staff of two! We saw over seventy additions in fewer than three years - in a supposedly "hard" mission field. Along with generous help from the disciples in Los Angeles and Eugene, Oregon, God used leadership from the London Church to gather and sustain remnant group churches in Kinshasa, Congo; Addis Ababa, Ethiopia; and Kiev, Ukraine.

This is what the next level looks like! Wow! Such a stunning and vivacious couple - the Williamsons, leaders of the Europe World Sector!

---

[2] £ is the symbol for the British currency: the pound sterling
[3] 2007 conversion rate

After two-and-a-half years of miracle-working, God moved through the City of Angels International Christian Church to send a mission team of ten disciples, led by Michael and Michele Williamson, to refresh the church in London and take it to the next level. Lianne and I went on to Los Angeles to continue our ministry training and embark upon our next adventure together. However, we will always be grateful for all the miracles that God did in London to advance the ministry and our little band of faithful warriors. It was at this time that I became convinced that wrestling for miracles was a critical element in Christian ministry.

When people see miracles, they build their confidence in God. As we see here at the Red Sea, *"...when the Israelites saw the mighty hand of the Lord displayed against the Egyptians, the people feared the Lord and put their trust in Him and in Moses His servant."* (Exodus 14:31) Miracles have always deeply moved God's people.

What else do miracles do? We see through the example above that miracles not only build people's confidence in God, but they also accredit God's leaders. We see this again in Acts 2:22, when the Apostle Peter preaches, *"Fellow Israelites, listen to this: Jesus of Nazareth was a man accredited by God to you by miracles, wonders and signs, which God did among you through Him, as you yourselves know."* At every juncture, God continues to use miracles to accredit His servants and His will for His people. God has always used miracles to help His people know the way that He wants them to go and whom He wants them to follow. It does not mean that people will automatically follow, but miracles help to clarify who God's leader is.

> *But when you enter a town and are not welcomed, go into its streets and say, "Even the dust of your town we wipe from our feet as a warning to you. Yet be sure of*

this: The Kingdom of God has come near." I tell you, it will be more bearable on that day for Sodom than for that town. "Woe to you, Chorazin! Woe to you, Bethsaida! For if the miracles that were performed in you had been performed in Tyre and Sidon, they would have repented long ago, sitting in sackcloth and ashes." (Luke 10:10-13)

People who want to do things for God will follow those through whom God works… and they better! In other words, when the church and the lost see the miracles of the change in the lives of those we are discipling, when they see us effectively baptizing at an inspiring tempo and growing spiritually (among other miracles listed below), they start to have no excuse but to recognize our godly leadership. They also begin to develop a godly fear. The Scripture above indicates that if they refuse to follow our leadership they could be in grave spiritual danger. Both the lost and the saved are thirsty for leadership, and we need to be God's leaders in the situation and work the miracles that lead the way! So many people are simply waiting for an authentic leader from God to follow.

> *"True spiritual leaders work miracles and rely on God's power!"*

Another thing miracles do is powerfully advance our ministry! A leader who tries to advance his or her ministry on their strength alone will find themselves burnt out and defeated. It is true that even miracles take "power" from us (Mark 5:30); but the Bible clearly says, **"Cursed is the one who trusts in man, who depends on flesh for his strength and whose heart turns away from the Lord."** (Jeremiah 17:5) This is an important mindset we must have. We cannot burn out by going on our own strength! True spiritual leaders work miracles and rely on God's power!

But how do we work miracles? We can work miracles because God makes Himself vulnerable to us. He will listen to us, bless us, and even change His plans for us (Genesis 18:28)! However, *"You do not have because you do not ask God. When you ask, you do not receive, because you ask with wrong motives, that you may spend what you get on your pleasures."* (James 4:2-3) God makes miracles happen when we are grateful (Colossians 3:16-17); when we ask for them consistently and passionately, God will give us whatever we are focused on for Him (Matthew 7:7); when we have pure hearts and good motives; when we pray (Mark 9:29); when we fast and weep (Esther 4:3); when we dream of them (Acts 2:17); when we take the right actions out of faith (James 2:24); and when we preach them into existence! (Genesis 1:3) Just like Jacob and Jesus, we must wrestle with God to see the amazing miracles happen.

Andrew Johnson (now a House Church Leader in the mighty South Region) is baptized in Los Angeles, California.

Today we live in a post-apostolic world where miracles no longer come with the laying on of hands and massive supernatural outpourings. In God's mercy and power, He has already accredited the ministry of Jesus and the early church through amazing miracles. The accreditation through miraculous signs in the first century was so powerful that even two thousand years later it is known to every living person with even a passing knowledge of religion. God is still doing miracles today! What are some of the miracles that will accredit and advance our ministries? Here are six miracles that need to blossom:

James Mitchell is baptizing his mother into Christ!

1. Baptisms: The greatest miracle of all time was the death, burial and resurrection of Jesus. However, what was the purpose of that miracle? It was to pay for the sins of humanity and allow the barrier of sin that separates man and God to be torn down. What is the fruit of that miracle? The salvation of our souls. How, exactly, do they come to God? They need to *"repent and be baptized"* (Acts 2:38), and in doing so, they die with Christ so that they can be raised to a new life! (Romans 6:2-4) Biblical baptism is not merely symbolic but the actual sharing by faith in the death, burial and resurrection of Jesus. Indeed, this is the point in time our new life begins!

43

2. Restorations: Satan has been deceiving people for thousands of years, and he has been seeking to pull Christians away from their faith since the birth of the church. Sadly, he sometimes succeeds. As disciples, we will always seek to restore our fallen brothers and sisters back to the faith. When people see their old fallen away friends come back to the faith, it accredits our ministry in an incredible way. We have snatched someone from the flames and brought them back into the Kingdom. (Jude 22-23) Restorations are an incredible miracle of God (James 5:19), because they free captive souls from the Kingdom of Darkness deliver them into the Kingdom of Light.

3. Repentance: Nothing hits a fellowship like broken-hearted, godly grace-inspired repentance. It is God who grants repentance. (2 Timothy 2:25) We do not deserve repentance, as many believe, and disciples of Christ must struggle against sin. Every disciple has their "Goliath" that needs to be slain by the "rock" of faith. As we disciple our few and train our small groups, lives change for the better and people grow in their relationships with God. As one sin after another is confessed and repented from - light, oxygen and growth replace the darkness and suffocation of mediocrity and defeat. (Acts 19:13-20)

4. Leaders Raising Up: One thing that Jesus focused on in His three-year ministry was making Apostles. (Mark 3:13) When formerly unmotivated, unreliable and unqualified men and women become great Bible Talk Leaders, preachers, disciplers, shepherds, deacons, web-deacons, children's ministry workers and giving servants in the church, people see God working. The miracle of raising up new leaders advances the ministry powerfully. (Acts 4:13)

5. Contribution and Special Contribution: When a godly leader leads churches, they dig deeper and sacrifice more. (2 Chronicles 11:16) At first, it is hard for them, because sacrifice is painful.

Churches need to be shown the need to hire Interns and support world missions; they must be called to greatness and inspired to sacrifice and be generous! (1 Timothy 6:18) It is counter-intuitive to think that sacrificing more will make disciples more committed; however, the Bible says clearly, *"For where your treasure is, there will your heart be also."* (Matthew 6:21)

6. Dating, Marriage and Family Healing: When disciples stay pure and date only disciples (Nehemiah 10:30; 1 Corinthians 6:14), the miracle of love rejuvenates the whole church! When families come back together in Christ, it is clearly the work of God! These are powerful miracles that need to happen in our ministries. Unhappy families and terrible relationships are not the calling card of God's chosen man or woman.

**Jake and Megan Studer on their joyful wedding
day in New York City in 2012!**

We need to call everyone in our ministry to be a miracle worker! Let us instill in every disciple these powerful convictions and watch the spectacular fireworks of miracles explode in our ministry and in the

Heavens! How hard do we need to wrestle for miracles? I will answer with a quote from Micheal Williamson leader of the London International Christian Church and the European World Sector, "How bad do you want it?"

Conviction 3:
Sort Out The "Shenanigans"

The church is a "refugee camp," in a world of chaos, sin and pain. Every ministry starts out in the honeymoon of joy and unity, but Satan's playbook is to stop growth with bitterness, discord, division and contempt. The time comes in every ministry where the "shenanigans" need to be engaged so forward advancement can continue.

Leaders committed to the standards of discipleship: The Kirchners, Bordieris, Kernans, McKeans and Untalans.

"The reason I left you in Crete was that you might put in order what was left unfinished..." (Titus 1:5)

47

Most groups - ministries, churches and even movements - start out as an idealistic group of people who want to share their faith and win souls. However, Satan's playbook is to sow division, discord and contempt until disillusionment replaces idealism and energetic evangelistic advancement grinds to a halt. This is when people become more occupied with the "shenanigans"[4] in the group than with reaching the lost. Satan can turn a ministry into a very unpleasant and unhealthy place to be. However, as we will see in this chapter, God has given us the playbook to engage and deal with Satan's schemes - the Bible! We must always get back to seeking and saving the lost!

In the Scripture below we find the genesis of New Testament shepherding and a rather startling description of the New Testament church. Paul goes into detail as to the qualifications of a shepherd or elder from verse five to eight. However, many people neglect to understand the "why" of shepherding. Let us pick up this letter on verse nine:

> *He must hold firmly to the trustworthy message as it has been taught, so that he can encourage others by sound doctrine and refute those who oppose it.*
>
> *For there are many rebellious people, mere talkers and decievers, especially those of the circumcision group. They must be silenced, because they are ruining whole households by teaching things they ought not to teach... Therefore, rebuke them sharply, so that they will be sound in the faith...* (Titus 1:9-13, NIV 1984 Abridged)

---

[4] *Shenanigan. noun she·nan·i·gan \shə-'na-ni-gən\ tricky or questionable practices or conduct - usually used in plural...mischievous activity - usually used in plural - Merriam Webster Dictionary*

This is a clear call to raise up leaders who can both encourage with sound doctrine and refute those who resist it. The Scriptures do not say that a Shepherd must "try" to refute, but actually refute! Paul is raising a militia of "minutemen" who will protect the nascent church from subversionaries who would tear it apart.

> *"The Scriptures do not say that a Shepherd must 'try' to refute, but actually refute!"*

He describes the New Testament church in Crete as a place with **"many rebellious people"** and orders that they **"be silenced"** before they ruin whole households! This goes against the "quaint" but misleading ideas many of us may have of a utopian first century church. Much like a body must constantly fight off infections to remain healthy, the church was constantly fighting off false doctrine and destructive practices.

"Silencing" people goes against the democratic flavor of our present age. Many believe that people should be able to share their feelings and thoughts, even if they are unhelpful to the unity and harmony of the church! Passive, apathetic or resigned acquiescence to sin is simply not compatible with the standard of the Bible. Certain attitudes, such as contempt, are not tolerated in the church, and apathy on our part as leaders should never be mistaken for maturity.

> **The man who shows contempt for the judge or for the priest who stands ministering there to the Lord your God must be put to death. You must purge the evil from Israel. All the people will hear and be afraid, and will not be contemptuous again.** (Deuteronomy 17:12-13)

While we do not live in the Old Testament era, we do have the same God, and His message about the gravity of contempt is mirrored by Paul and other writers of the New Testament. In Hebrews 12:14-15, we see a similar message:

> *Make every effort to live in peace with everyone and to be holy; without holiness no one will see the Lord. See to it that no one falls short of the grace of God and that no bitter root grows up to cause trouble and defile many.*

As per this Scripture, it is the responsibility of every disciple to *"see to it... that no root of bitterness"* take hold in the church and dishonor our family. This can take the form of discord, dissensions or factions to name only a few. Defilement fouls a childlike heart, which is necessary to enter the Kingdom of God (Matthew 18:3), and causes us to sink us into bickering and quarreling. Bitterness takes away holiness and so becomes a salvation issue. It is not loving or caring to allow a brother or sister to continue in bitterness without calling for repentance. The Scripture teaches in 2 Timothy 2:22-26:

> *And the Lord's servant must not be quarrelsome but must be kind to everyone, able to teach, not resentful. Opponents must be gently instructed, in the hope that God will grant them repentance leading them to a knowledge of the truth, and that they will come to their senses and escape from the trap of the devil, who has taken them captive to do his will.*

We are called to an incredibly high standard as disciples in the Kingdom of God! We must never quarrel but must be kind, pleasant and able to teach even when we have been hurt. Repeat these words often in lessons, *"...kind to everyone, able to teach, not resentful..."* Marcus Aurelius, Emperor of Rome, once said "When you wake up in the morning, tell yourself: The people I deal with today will be meddling, ungrateful, arrogant, dishonest, jealous, and surly. They are like this because they can't tell good from evil... No one can implicate me in ugliness. Nor can I feel angry at my relative, or hate him. We were born to work together like feet, hands, and eyes, like the two rows of teeth, upper and lower. To obstruct each other is unnatural." Teaching people to have character and understand the importance of working together is so important. We are commanded to "silence" rebellion (Titus 1:9-13) and the best possible way to "silence" bitterness or subversiveness is to teach people how to deal with their hurts and trepidations constructively.

We cannot allow our hurts to become fuel for resentments or bitterness. Not only Paul but also Jesus gives us clear direction on how to solve our conflicts and offenses.

> *If your brother or sister sins, go and point out their fault, just between the two of you. If they listen to you, you have won them over. But if they will not listen, take one or two others along, so that "every matter may be established by the testimony of two or three witnesses." If they still refuse to listen, tell it to the church; and if they refuse to listen even to the church, treat them as you would a pagan or a tax collector.* (Matthew 18:15-17)

While Matthew 18 is a very basic Scripture that many know, it is often overlooked or poorly practiced. We must be the healers and solvers, the doctor who cures cancer, not the lab tech who points it out. This is the Christian standard and the only way to keep the refugee camp, which is the church, a safe place.

How do good Christians become the *"rebellious people"* (Titus 1:9-13) as Paul describes? Very often people can simply be afraid of being hurt and fail to have faith in the promises of God. (Jeremiah 29:11, Romans 8:28) Others can be hurt and fail in their responsibility to handle their problems in a Biblical manner. Still others have simply never been part of a family and are coming into the Kingdom "feral," needing to be trained in how to operate together in a loving family. In all these cases, and countless others, Satan can take hold of people and begin to use them to harm God's church.

On the other hand some people are less *"rebellious"* as much as they are on a pendulum swing in their lives. *"It is true that some preach Christ out of envy and rivalry, but others out of goodwill. The latter do so out of love, knowing that I am put here for the defense of the Gospel. The former preach Christ out of selfish ambition, not sincerely..."* (Philippians 1:15-17) These are the kind of people who will seek to climb the "corporate ladder" of the church regardless of who they may hurt on the way. They must be taught that we are not here to build "great churches" or "great ministries." We are here as revolutionaries to change the world. Only then do we look around occasionally and take note that we truly are in great churches and ministries! Often these selfishly ambitious people, if they do not repent, will pendulum swing at some point in their life to become *"...a stiff-necked people."* (Exodus 32:9) They dig their heels in at all direction from leadership and justify it under the pretense of being "super spiritual." Satan catches many well intentioned people in these traps.

People who struggle with these pretentions must be reminded that we are a *"... a chosen people, a royal priesthood, a holy nation, God's special possession..."* (1 Peter 2:9) We must be princes and princesses in the Kingdom of God. Not selfishly ambitious but simply happy to be a member of the true family. You can never find out how God feels about you from your title or role. You can only learn your worth from the cross. On the other hand, understanding our place as princes and princesses means we cannot have our "heels dug in," but must be eager and happy to serve in any capacity in our Fathers house.

Many people who have been through a serious rebellion - like the fall of the ICOC - can come out of the experience deeply scarred. The trauma and fear, if unhealed, becomes a lens through which they see all ministry. They believe the only solution to rebellion is surrender to it. They believe it is best never to do anything or call anyone to do anything, which could ever lead to bitterness or rebellion. This is a paralyzing leadership style that leads to all kinds of sin. It leads to the backing off the Biblical principles of centralized visionary leadership and overseeing evangelists (Numbers 27:13-20; 1 Corinthians 4:17), discipleship, sacrifice, standards, etc. It is a cynical, humanistic, two-dimensional perspective without a Biblical foundation or the light of God's wisdom. For many, it is more of a feeling than perspective. They cringe at bold or dramatic visionary leadership that might stir up resentment. They begin to think that it is the leadership that they must fight and forget that Satan is their real enemy. (Ephesians 6:12)

On the other hand, we should not be cavalier and think people will be added to our ministry and just sit there and happily produce forever. People power is one of the hardest forms of energy to channel. Revolutions and overthrows have shaped modern history more than any other factor. If we think we will not deal with the explosive force of "people power," we are naïve at best. If we just want to add members and refuse to "sort out the shenanigans," our name will merely be added to the long list of those who ignored these dangers. In the words of Cicero, "No tempest or conflagration, however great, is harder to quell than mob carried away by the novelty of power." He would know!

Question: Why do leaders always seem to be the target? Answer: Once Satan takes down the leaders, then the flock becomes easy pickings. God uses leaders to provide direction and unity, without which the church is defenseless. A nation without leaders is easy to enslave. Therefore, it is often leaders who take the brunt of the battle to keep the church a unified and loving place.

> *Have confidence in your leaders and submit to their authority, because they keep watch over you as those who must give an account. Do this so that their work will be a joy, not a burden, for that would be of no benefit to you.* (Hebrews 13:17)

And again:

> *Now we ask you, brothers and sisters, to acknowledge those who work hard among you, who care for you in the Lord and who admonish you.* (1 Thessalonians 5:12)

Even when we are *"putting [a ministry] in order,"* we must stay evangelistic! Remember, Satan's mission is to stop the evangelistic advancement of the church! A bee can make honey, but it also has a stinger! Do not be all stinger and no honey - or vice versa!

Have confidence as you keep the church safe and know that God is with you.

> *These are the words of Him who holds the seven stars in His right hand and walks among the seven golden lampstands. I know your deeds, your hard work and your perseverance. I know that you cannot tolerate wicked people, that you have tested those who claim to be Apostles but are not, and have found them false. You have persevered and have endured hardships for*

my name, and have not grown weary. (Revelations 2:1-3)

Jesus commends the church for their stand on discipleship and standards. "A surgeon does not hesitate to remove a limb or an organ to preserve life..."[5] and when the time comes to see someone leave the fellowship of believers, we should not be hesitant. The battle against bitterness and rebellion is one that will never cease. We, as leaders, must be absolutely comfortable "sorting out the shenanigans" and be able to switch fluidly to the rest of our duties without any sign of favoring one task over the other. The resurrected Jesus is watching.

I remember in 2006 flying into war-torn Kinshasa, the Democratic Republic of Congo, for the first time. I had been sent to solidify a group of disciples who wished to join our movement of churches. This was before the elections that were scheduled, and there was considerable insecurity throughout the city. In fact, the airport itself was under the control of militia groups and of starving, desperate employees. All the other passengers on the airplane disembarked quickly and boarded cars and trucks to leave the area immediately. Ignorant of these dangers, I entered the airport looking for a taxi.

I was quickly mugged by a mishmash of "security" personnel and hungry, desperate employees. It was a terrifying experience to be so far from home and so helpless. I did have the option to get back on the plane, but something told me to keep going on my mission - to encourage the fledgling church there.

A militiaman with a barely functioning Jeep offered to take me to a hotel where he told me there were journalists. He charged me an

---

[5] Bruce C. Birch, Walter Brueggemann, David L. Peterson and Terence E. Frethem, *A Theological Introduction to the Old Testament*. ISBN: 0687013488

exorbitant sum of $100 USD for the short drive, but I was grateful to pay it. As we headed into Kinshasa, the fear in my heart was blown into flames as I saw the throngs of starving, barely clothed people crowded on both sides of the street. It was more than my senses could bear. We passed by a United Nations base guarded by blue-helmeted soldiers, and I ordered the Jeep to stop. As a former infantryman in the Canadian Army, I knew the safety and security I would enjoy inside that camp.

I looked over at the base longingly. However, again, I chose to keep going to the hotel so that I could contact the church. Only God gave me the courage.

Looking at that UN base from the chaos of the street was an epiphany for me. It became a spiritual illustration for what the church should be. The poverty and bedlam of the street contrasted sharply with the order and security of the UN base. This image was permanently etched into my mind. The restrained, yet capable-looking peacekeepers who guarded the camp, became an image for me of leaders guarding the church.

Just as Nehemiah cried when he heard about the broken walls and gates of Jerusalem (Nehemiah 1:4), I saw more clearly than ever that the church needs men and women willing to build a wall comprised of the standards of discipleship and defend it against attack. The wall defines and protects the church from the terrors that wait outside. When standards in the church are broken, the wall is broken, and "the enemy" can enter and raise havoc. When they are well defended, the church is radiant. Our wall is not of stone but living stones (1 Peter 2:5), which are the disciples themselves.

Remember, a wall may look strong, a disciple may seem committed, but we must ensure that they are. Like parasites, false teachers bury themselves and their teaching in the church (2 Peter 2:1), and it is only when we begin calling everyone to Christ's standards that they start to agitate against us. That is why both calling our ministries to the standards of Christ and confronting bitterness, contempt and discord are inseparable topics.

"The Kingdom of Heaven is like treasure hidden in a field. When a man found it, he hid it again, and then in his joy went and sold all he had and bought that field." (Matthew 13:44) One of the famous terms used by many great leaders I know when referring to a Christian who is completely committed, dedicated and devoted to the standards of Christ is "sold-out!" We often hear: *"That guy is sold out!"* As a result, in 2007 Kip and Elena officially gave our movement the name "The SoldOut Movement." As Ricky Challinor says "you are either sold out or on your way out!"

When we are calling people to be sold-out for Jesus' standards, false teachers will always find a way to make it appear that our Biblical standards are actually just our personal preferences or stylistic choices. While it is true that so much of everyday ministry is more art than science, the standards are not debatable. The attacks of persecutors and false teachers, of course, are not directed against the teaching of Jesus but us personally. We need to deal wisely and patiently, but also decisively, with those who actively oppose the standards of Christ. Some false teachers are completely conscious of what they are doing, but their greed and resentment drive them on. Others are deceived and will therefore deceive others. *"But there were also false prophets among the people, just as there will be false teachers among you. They will secretly introduce destructive heresies..."* (2 Peter 2:1-3) We need to stay close to God and not take these attacks personally. This is how all the prophets were treated before us. (Luke 6:23) We can take comfort that we are part of a Heavenly fraternity.

Not only must we have a thick skin, but we must have a love for God and for people so strong that we will not shy away from any fight to save a soul. ***"Or again, how can anyone enter a strong man's house and carry off his possessions unless he first ties up the strong man? Then he can plunder his house."*** (Matthew 12:29) As we see in this Scripture… it will always be a fight. The ***"strong man"*** in the passage is Satan, and he must be tied up before we can "steal" souls from his dominion.

This takes a spiritual fight or "violence" and a real commitment to saving a soul. In the words of famous American author Robert A. Heinlein, "Anyone who clings to the historically untrue - and thoroughly immoral - doctrine that 'violence never settles anything' I would advise to conjure the ghosts of Napoleon Bonaparte and the Duke of Wellington and let them debate it. The ghost of Hitler could referee, and the jury might well be the Dodo bird, and the Passenger Pigeon. Violence, naked force, has settled more issues in history than has any other factor, and the contrary opinion is wishful thinking at its worst. [Kingdoms] that forget this basic truth have always paid for it with their lives and their freedom."

It must become a deep conviction that problems do not go away "on their own." Faithful, prayerful leaders must engage them. Christianity does not need mere thinkers but warriors. As Thucydides once wrote, "The nation that makes a great distinction between its scholars and its warriors will have its thinking done by cowards and its fighting done by fools." The church deserves much more. Problems only multiply when we fail to engage them faithfully. Remember, a cavity never goes away; if it is not given a filling early on, then a root canal will be in order. If we fail to get a root canal, then we may lose the tooth. This must become second nature in your thinking. The problem you avoid today will be worse tomorrow if left unattended. We need to go in the strength we have to protect the church! (Judges 6:14) Keep the "fight" in our thinking and practice of the ministry life. We must not start believing this is just another white-collar job… it is not.

Indeed, we can never avoid the fight to keep the church pure, regardless of the cost. *"He is the one we proclaim, admonishing and teaching everyone with all wisdom, so that we may present everyone fully mature in Christ. To this end I strenuously contend with all the energy Christ so powerfully works in me."* (Colossians 1:28-29) We need to keep our motivations pure and fight with a happy heart and a peaceful spirit. As we work to present everyone perfect, remember that Christ is going to give us energy. Pray to God for the energy, enthusiasm and determination to deal with the issues He puts in our lives. (Hebrews 12:7) Failing to do so may mean giving up on our lives and freedom down the road.

When we start talking about standards, some feel that it smacks of "earning" one's salvation. The truth is that we do not "earn" anything by being a disciple. However, if we want to "come after Jesus" (Matthew 16:34), then discipleship is the only way to enter His fellowship and the only acceptable response to His offer of grace. Our attitude must be this:

> *Suppose one of you has a servant plowing or looking after the sheep. Will he say to the servant when he comes in from the field, "Come along now and sit down to eat?" Won't he rather say, "Prepare my supper, get yourself ready and wait on me while I eat and drink; after that you may eat and drink?" Will he thank the servant because he did what he was told to do? So you also, when you have done everything you were told to do, should say, "We are unworthy servants; we have only done our duty."* (Luke 17: 7-10)

The Scriptures are clear: Being a disciple - and doing the work that is entailed in being one - does not earn us anything in Heaven. It is only our duty. A disciple of Jesus understands these principles. A true disciple is not only committed to following Jesus' standards but also calls everyone else who has made Jesus his or her Lord and Savior to the same standards - even if it means being persecuted.

Alfredo Anuch has done incredible things with the mighty Santiago, Chile ICC. He is a true Nehemiah in our day!

Basic principle aside, here are a few nuances to "sorting out the shenanigans":

As leaders, we know that timing is critical. There is a reason that this principle is third, after "focus on the few" and "wrestle for miracles." If there are no "few" and there are no "miracles," then it is very hard to apply this principle and teaching. When we approach those who are obviously not attaining the standards of discipleship, we must have an example to call them to and accreditation as a leader from God. While it is natural to think that if everyone in our ministries were living up to the standards, the ministry would do very well. That logic is true, but it is in achieving this situation that we make our mistakes. We must lead a ministry to greatness. We must draw out a committed few, we must wrestle for the miracles that accredit us and advance our ministry, and then, when our lives light a clear path, we can call everyone else to walk down that path with us. Merely being critical of those who are uncommitted does not get the job done. Abraham Lincoln once said, "Give me six hours to chop down a tree, and I will spend the first four sharpening the ax." We need to take our time and get it right the first time - every time.

Not only is "timing" critical, but also just plain old time. I love John 10:3-5 because it shows the value of relationship and trust in leadership. *"He calls his own sheep by name and leads them out. When he has brought out all his own, he goes on ahead of them, and his sheep follow him because they know his voice. But they will never follow a stranger; in fact, they will run away from him because they do not recognize a stranger's voice."* While there is no excuse to fail to call our membership to the standards of Christ, the deeper our relationships, the more successful we will be in establishing the standards in our ministry! This is a powerful principle to remember. In Los Angeles in 2016, we implemented "Project Shepherds' Voice," which was an effort to keep region leaders in place longer so they could bond more with the people and the people would feel more secure in their relationship with their leaders.

Timing and time do not make up for lack of knowledge. Nehemiah *"[surveyed] the wall"* (Nehemiah 2:13) before he engaged in the building. Proverbs 27:23 exhorts us to make sure we know the condition of our flocks. We must work hard to get the necessary information, and build a great plan before we engage in "sorting out the shenanigans." We must also be prepared to adjust and rethink our plan as new information comes to us.

Hector Gomez is a preacher with a deep love for the lost, especially fallen away Christians. His inspiring preaching will continue to gather many back into the flock of God!

As we wade into the battle, it is always a great idea to have a "reach back" group of experienced ministers who are respected friends from whom we can receive support and seek advice. Sometimes a good sounding board makes the difference between good "sound" decisions and bad ones. One way to fumble in "sorting out the shenanigans" is to fail to seek advice and bring in other concerned leaders. By failing to "get our ducks in a row," we can create blowouts in which people whom we are trying to address go "around us" and misinform other leaders as to our intentions. It sounds like high school, but this can create friction between us and our peers that will be counterproductive. It might even be a good idea to allow our shepherds or mature disciples to engage the issues at hand first, and only involve ourselves if it is an issue which is "over their heads." If we do not have shepherds then we must select, train and appoint them. (Titus 1:5-11)

Often, because more mature disciples have been under attack from Satan much longer, they may need more support. (Hebrews 2:1) We must be very wise and gracious as we treat these disciples the way the Bible commands, *"Stand up in the presence of the aged, show respect for the elderly and revere your God. I am the Lord."* (Leviticus 19:32) This does not mean that we should fail to confront their sin; it simply means that we need to be very respectful in doing so with older disciples. To become effective at this very difficult "art" of confronting an older disciple, it is imperative that you observe an older disciple graciously engage an issue. *"Do not rebuke an older man harshly, but exhort Him as if he were your father."* (1 Timothy 5:1) Regardless of the truth of our cause, if we approach older disciples without the respect they deserve and expect, then our efforts will be derailed before we even begin. We can create a rebellion by our tone and manner as much as by what we say. We need to train ourselves to "talk up" to older disciples, even if we are admonishing them, even if we are *"over them in the Lord."* (1 Thessalonians 5:12) This is a crucial issue that takes much prayer, advice, Scriptural insight and practice.

At the other end of the spectrum are our campus ministries. So many campus ministries have been taken down by sin. (Psalm 25:7) Although campus ministries have the potential to grow dramatically because of youthful idealism, they also have the potential to be taken down just as quickly because of the *"evil desires of youth."* (2 Timothy 2:22) Calling disciples to have the ideals of the Bible as their standards is as vital in the campus ministry as anywhere else in the church.

Regardless of age or role, we as leaders must be masters of subtlety, restraint, timing and accuracy when the time comes to engage a situation and deliver a rebuke. *"Through patience a ruler can be persuaded, and a gentle tongue can break a bone."* (Proverbs 25:15)

> *"Half of our battles will be won not by the sword, but with the plowshare and the pruning hook."*

People can drift from the standards simply because of a lack of fruit. When John the Baptist began wavering and questioning his commitment to the cause, *"Jesus replied, 'Go back and report to John what you hear and see: The blind receive sight, the lame walk, those who have leprosy are cleansed, the deaf hear, the dead are raised, and the good news is proclaimed to the poor.'"* (Matthew 11:4) There is no way to overemphasize that half the battle of calling the church to the standards and winning everyone over to unity is by wrestling for the miracle of baptisms. A fruitful disciple or church is most often a fully committed and happy disciple or church. As such, half of our battles will be won not by the sword, but with the plowshare and the pruning hook. Even in the world, there are rarely rebellions in rich and productive countries. We need to choose the plowshare over the sword wherever we have the chance.

It is worth considering that when we are calling people to the standards, we first ensure that they have convictions on the standards and have been taught how to attain them! As my discipler Kip has often said, "The cardinal sin of discipling is assuming." We always need to start out by teaching and inspiring people to attain

Jesus' standards. We then set goals for them and encourage them to "get back on the horse" if they falter. Not everyone who is falling short is rebellious or lazy; they may simply be ignorant. It is not without reason that the Bible says that the Scriptures are **"useful for teaching, rebuking, correcting and training"** so that we are thoroughly equipped for good work. (2 Timothy 3:16-17) We cannot expect people to do what we have not trained them to do!

**The City of Angels International Christian Church
Leadership received certificates after graduating
from the First Principles Class!**

Always remember that the value of a refugee camp is not in its size but its quality. Consider another analogy: Does a country get richer by simply printing more money? Indeed, it can become suddenly much poorer. We need to protect the "currency" of church membership and its value by assuring ourselves that every member of each Bible Talk is, indeed, a true disciple. Countries that print meaningless "fiat currency" eventually face financial collapse. Churches that baptize people before they are ready, and fail to call people to the standard are printing worthless memberships forms. We need to consider the strength of the currency of membership in our ministry!

One mistake often made in dealing with sin or opposition is "half-dealing" with the issue. For example, it may become clear that we need to engage a brother's or sister's heart because of outward symptoms that start to affect the rest of the church. However, instead of staying on task, we can drop the matter when the outward symptoms disappear. This can result in a much worse problem next time.

By "half-dealing" with the issue - which is not dealing with the issue at all - we may be creating weak points in the protective "walls" of our ministry that become even harder to repair the next time. It is vital to go all the way to the heart of the matter the first time, rebuilding the walls solidly and not just engaging the symptoms and outward actions. How do we do that? Acts 20:26 tells us that deeds must prove true repentance. All involved should be able to see and know that repentance has occurred. We need to be sure to set up follow-up meetings, talk to the people who have been affected by the situation and remember that where we find one issue we usually find two. We may need to immunize or "fireproof" the ministry through solid Biblical preaching, teaching and specific direction.

The Kernans, Thomases, Johnsons and Rajans celebrating the appointment of the Johnsons and Thomases as Shepherds-in-Training in Chennai in 2013.

Having a healthy and happy church is not about a periodical "house-cleaning" strategy. That style of leadership can create more disruption and disturbance than the lack of standards. Maintaining standards is about persistence and presence. Stay close and stay for good. People will usually side with the leader who is closer physically and who can spend more time with them. If we cannot be that person, then we should not be the one to win them over just to see them fall again. We cannot go anywhere where we will not either stay or commit ourselves to leaving effective and loyal leadership behind. Otherwise, people will feel like a soccer ball and will eventually get fatigued because of the constant "to and fro." When we go into a ministry, we need to get in close to the people and let them know that we and the leaders we train and leave behind will be there for them for the long haul.

Practically, this is done by organizing our fellowship into strong Bible Talks. (More on this in "Conviction 5: Get Them Leading Small Groups.") This allows us to spend time with a small, easy-to-manage group. This gives us relationships where we can raise up visionary leadership who will keep the Bible Talk strong, and then we can move on to the next Bible Talk secure in the knowledge that we are leaving a strong group behind. By pursuing this methodology, we are taking the initiative and pushing toward the end goal of a unified and committed church. We should never take on a group only as a whole, but mainly through Bible Talks. Without organized Bible Talks and the raising up of strong leadership at that level, we cannot be successful. For example, if we have a church of 80 that must be "put in order," (Titus 1:5) we should start by forming eight to 10 small groups. From experience, if we can put in order four or five of them, then the others will often fall in line on their own. *"The man who shows contempt... must be put to death. You must purge the evil from Israel. All the people will hear and be afraid, and will not be contemptuous again."* (Deuteronomy 17:12-13) With this method, one or two ministers can engage any size group.

"When a country is rebellious, it has many rulers, but a ruler with discernment and knowledge maintains order." (Proverbs 28:2) Every ministry must have clear leadership. Sometimes conflict happens in the church because there are too many "chefs in the

kitchen." In nature storms emerge when two air masses of dissimilar temperature and humidity clash. The greater the difference, the greater the storm. The storm will continue until the difference is resolved. A hot leader will lead to a hot church and a hot church in a cold world will always be surrounded by storm. If there is no storm the church has succumb to the cold. We cannot just think about symptoms, but always consider root causes.

Sometimes the issues we must engage have less to do with bringing the church to the standards of Christ than with straightforward security and safety. Sexual predators love welcoming churches to lurk in, as do con-artists. We should keep our eyes peeled and our ears to the ground for these dangers to our flock. When we find false brothers or sisters like this, we must bring matters to the right authorities and deal with them quickly. We are the guarantors of the safety of the church. The flock, not to mention God, has an expectation that we will even lay our lives down for their safety if necessary. Anything that threatens or endangers the church is the leadership's business be it sexual predators, false doctrine, financial issues or anything else.

Just from reading the Pauline Epistles, we might think that a large portion of the work of a leader is to bring order to the chaotic tenancies of the church. While true, this goes against the democratic views of our era. Conversely, one of the most classic of mistakes that leaders can make is to "overplay our cards." When we have a powerful "few" and the accreditation of God through miracles in the ministry, in our excitement, we can sometimes be tempted to become harsh, arrogant and scornful towards those who do not attain the standards. Having a critical eye and mind can be a great benefit for a leader, but some have let their critical eye "drip down" and give them a critical heart. Once you become frustrated with someone you are handicapping your ability to help them change.

If we are harsh in dealing with wrongdoing in the church, we can conjure up support for the wrongdoer because people will feel sympathy for the way they are being treated. False teachers may take advantage of the situation by then positioning themselves as victims of our "over-righteous zealotry and mean-hearted legalism." This can cloud the issues at stake and leave us with false teaching plus division to manage. While firm and unapologetic, our raising of the church must be done by calling for imitation (1 Thessalonians 1:6), with **"great patience and careful instruction"** (2 Timothy 4:2), and with love and gentleness. (1 Thessalonians 2:7-8; 2 Timothy 2:24-26) It takes much prayer and the seeking of advice to get this right.

In other words, we cannot do a great job of building a safe and happy church, and then go too far and create a "police state." As it is written in the Scriptures, **"Do not pay attention to every word people say, or you may hear your servant cursing you - for you know in your heart that many times you yourself have cursed others."** (Ecclesiastes 7 21-22) Allow some things to filter through without engaging them. Only if they begin to repeat themselves do you know you must intervene.

We should never forget that opponents can be won over. As a disciple, we must believe that anyone can change and that anyone can grow. (2 Timothy 2:25) It might mean that we will need to "hug a prickly porcupine" to get him or her to lower their needles. It hurts, but it works! Abraham Lincoln once said, "I destroy my enemies when I make them my friends." We must accept risk and pain to avoid losing those who can be won over.

As Paul writes in 1 Timothy 1:3-7, **"As I urged you when I went into Macedonia, stay there in Ephesus so that you may command certain men not to teach false doctrines any longer... These promote controversies rather than God's work**

- which is by faith. The goal of this command is love, which comes from a pure heart and a good conscience and a sincere faith. " Bringing everyone in the ministry to the standards of Christ is not a matter of being mean, but of *"love, which comes from a pure heart and a good conscience and a sincere faith. "*

While we may or may not have set out to be masters of building the "family church," the overwhelming sense of family is the perhaps the counter intuitive byproduct and outcome of being "Titus 1:9-13" adherents - committed to protecting God's church. On the other hand beware that in presiding over a great "family church" you do not become inward focused and forget the mission!

John Adams once said, "I must study politics and war, that my sons may have the liberty to study mathematics and philosophy… in order to give their children the right to study painting, poetry and music." Although I do not believe that protecting the church is politics and war in the worldly sense, I can certainly empathize with the spirit of what John Adams is saying. I believe this to be true for most ministers. We fight so that our spiritual and physical children can live in peace and be happy.

Also, we need to know that our skill and readiness to engage the shenanigans will actually deter many from "messing around" in the first place. In the words of Ronald Reagan, the 40th President of the United States, "The most fundamental paradox is that, if we're never to use force, we must be prepared to use it and to use it successfully… If our efforts are successful, we will have peace and never be forced into battle." Evangelists who "sort out the shenanigans" are godly deterrence for sin in the flock. This is a new concept for the Restoration Movement that has always been torn to shreds by internal strife.

Ministry is not easy. It is good to have a thick skin, a few close friends, a great wife and enjoy the simple things. Whatever we do - we cannot give up. The consequences are too severe and the rewards too good! We must fight hard to build a church where others can come and have protection.

Is it time to "sort out the shenanigans" in our ministries? Do we have our few? Do miracles accredit us? Are we ready for what we might find as we set out to call our ministry to the standards? If so, then with prayerful humility and powerful resolve, we need to set out on our mission of love!

★★

In early 2007, my wife Lianne and I landed at Gatwick Airport in London to lead the London International Christian Church. Our visas had not yet been granted, the church incorporation and charity permits were not secured, and there were only four members of the church with about £1,500 ($3,000 USD) in the church bank account. Our worship service location was a small but warm living room in Poplar, near of the Isle of Dogs, which is situated in one of the poorest parts of London. In many ways, from a worldly point of view, it was a mission with very limited chances for success. However, in three years, that church rose to 31 members with five Bible Talks, sent out four leaders to support other churches, and had annual revenue of over $130,000 per year. (2007 conversion) Not only that, but we secured visas, incorporation and charity permits, as well as the right to hire foreign workers. This happened in the middle of a financial meltdown in the country and with an anti-immigration government in power.

As a result, a strong mission team from Los Angeles gallantly led by Michael and Michele Williamson was able to reinforce the disciples and successfully take the group to the next level at far less cost than if a church had to be planted from scratch.

The two major factors that I believe led to the multiplication of disciples and the success of that group were: 1) Inspiring as many as possible to become leaders of small groups; and 2) Creating strong unity. These two convictions became what I consider "fundamental factors" in the fortifying of any church. The third "fundamental" that I only learned later while training under Kip in Los Angeles to lead the Paris Mission Team, was the principle of "excellence." In Los Angeles, I learned the explosive power of doing things excellently. What I learned has had such an impact on me that I have added it to my list of fortifying convictions that need to be woven into the construction of any ministry.

We have our few; we have the miracles; we are ready for the battle to call the membership to the standards of Christ. Now it is time to dig in to fortify and strengthen our gains.

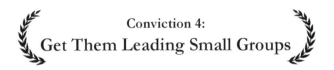

Conviction 4:
Get Them Leading Small Groups

Leaders are God's way to multiply His Kingdom. Small groups produce leaders. Inspiring and training your people to become leaders in your ministry is essential.

The 2015 Spring Semester Bachelor Class of the International College of Christian Ministries in Los Angeles.

As Jesus was walking beside the Sea of Galilee, He saw two brothers, Simon called Peter and his brother Andrew. They were casting a net into the lake, for they were fishermen. "Come, follow me," Jesus said, "and I will send you out to fish for people." At once they left their nets and followed Him. (John 4:18-20)

One of the most important things we do as leaders is make other leaders. We are "talent scouts" and our mission is not to make ourselves great, but to make others great. By inspiring people to become leaders, we increase our ability to reach progressively more people with the Gospel. As we see in the Scripture, when Jesus called disciples to follow Him, it was for the purpose of training them to be leaders and *"fishers of men."* (Matthew 4:19 NIV 1984)

When the disciples began to follow Jesus, He became, among other things, their "coach." He believed in them and would train them to achieve the goals that He set out for them. Jesus was not looking for someone who "wanted to get baptized." Rather, He was taking on Apostles whom He would train and send out. This is an essential thought and attitude to have.

In John 3:22, the Bible says, *"After this, Jesus and His disciples went out into the Judean countryside, where He spent some time with them, and baptized."* This is a perfect example of Jesus taking His new disciples out on their first expedition together. He was the main driver of the activities as He spent time with them. He also baptized in their presence - and probably with their participation - so that they could "learn the ropes" first-hand.

He stretched them evangelistically, but it is obvious when reading the Gospels that *"spending time with them"* in John 3:22 included teaching them all about how to worship God, to know the Scriptures, and to become the disciples that Jesus wanted them to be. This spending time and constantly talking about God and ministry is so important. As the Scripture says, *"Fix these words of mine in your hearts and minds; tie them as symbols on your hands and bind them on your foreheads. Teach them to your children, talking about them when you sit at home and when you walk along the road, when you lie down and when you get up. Write them on the doorframes of your houses and on your gates..."* (Deuteronomy 11:18-20) We rush ahead and skip this stage to our peril. Remember, if we are not having regular discipling times with our people, then Satan is.

Not only by spending time with Jesus, but also through their sometimes-stormy relationships with one another, they grew. *"As iron sharpens iron, so one person sharpens another."* (Proverbs 27:17) For Jesus, nothing was a coincidence or an inconvenience. Every conflict, or situation that arose among them, no matter how difficult or trivial, was an opportunity to train His disciples so they could grow. We need to follow that model today.

In Acts 4:13, even the Pharisees noticed the impact of Jesus spending time with His disciples: *"When they saw the courage of Peter and John and realized that they were unschooled, ordinary men, they were astonished and they took note that these men had been with Jesus."* Jesus' training model worked.

It is safe to say that without the training and practice the Apostles received - as I referred to above in John 3:22 - then the following in John 4:1-2 would never have happened. It reads, *"The Pharisees heard that Jesus was gaining and baptizing more disciples than John, although in fact it was not Jesus who baptized, but His disciples."* Here, Jesus' disciples have grown, and Jesus has shifted gears from baptizing with them to supervising them, as they have begun to baptize on their own. As the Greek thinker Archilochus once wrote, "We don't rise to the level of our expectations, we fall to the level of our training." The Apostles were expertly trained by watching Jesus baptize and then baptized while being supervised by Jesus.

He produced leaders who expanded and multiplied His work to reach even more people! This is an incredible outcome of Jesus' work. Jesus' ministry raised up effective leaders whom he later sent out. In fact, any successful Christian ministry is a ministry that builds and "exports" leaders. A sure sign of a ministry in trouble is a ministry that needs to "import" leaders from outside consistently.

> *"Someone who has the 'virus' of leadership and is a 'carrier' of that virus will infect those around them..."*

Someone who has the "virus" of leadership and is a "carrier" of that virus will "infect" those around them and turn them into leaders as well. Those without the "virus" or with a weak virus will fail to make leaders. The "virus" of leadership must be a deadly one. If we merely have the "flu" of leadership, we will only give people the sniffles. We must be a carrier of the "Ebola of leadership." People must die to themselves so that Jesus can live and lead through us. We need to be as infectious as possible!

By "taking His disciples to Judea" - by that we mean showing them the example and then switching to a supervisory role - Jesus built a simple ministry model that even those of us who are of lesser ability and stamina can copy. That being said, simple should not be confused with easy. Jesus trained His followers and then switched to a supervisory role at the perfect moment. It takes a lot of practice to get it right. Most of us need several run-ups.

One of the greatest examples of leadership-making in our generation is the International College of Christian Ministries (ICCM). The ICCM is a private Christian college, recognized by the State of California. The ICCM provides education and "on the job training" for the Ministry Staff of the SoldOut Movement.

As Lianne and I were preparing to take a mission team to Paris, France in early August 2012, we were wrestling with the difficulty of securing visas without degrees in ministry. Our Movement has always taught that the best and only way to become a leader is to walk with another leader for years. Therefore, most of us even those who had served the church for years, did not have recognized degrees in ministry or theology. It was during this time that the idea for the ICCM was born. This would accomplish a number of things. One is that it would provide missionaries with academic accreditation so they could secure visas more easily. Another thing it would do is provide a vehicle to accredit all the incredible training and work that our leaders already do and capture it all against a transcript. This way they could be awarded university diplomas! So many of our leaders had left college to pursue the ministry, and it would be amazing to see them finally receive degrees! Finally, it created a codified training for our Interns as they strived to become Evangelists and Women's Ministry Leaders.

Kip had made many efforts to do the same thing on several occasions in the ICOC; however, there was never unity as to how a college would be formed. My dear friend, Chris Adams, made the formal application to the California Bureau of Postsecondary Education. Everyone rejoiced on August 16, 2012, when they approved our application for the founding of the ICCM. Our "Verification of Exempt Status" allows the ICCM to grant Bachelors, Masters and Doctoral Degrees in Ministry according to our own Biblical doctrines and standards.

We were all excited as Kip gathered an amazing team of indispensable disciples to create the Bachelors, Masters and Doctorate Program. Included were: Dr. Elena Garcia McKean, Dr. Andrew Smellie, Dr. Kyle Bartholomew, Michael Kirchner, Chris Adams, Helen Sullivan and myself. We continued to believe that there was no substitute for walking with leaders to make leaders.

However, the ICCM was to add an academic element to "round out" our leaders' training.

It was agreed that an ICCM Bachelor of Arts Degree would be attained in one of two ways. First, by years of service as an appointed Evangelist, Women's Ministry Leader, Shepherding Couple, MERCY Director or Administrator. The second route is by going through the formal training sessions of the ICCM while working as an intern in the church.

For the Interns, their training program began by reading all 66 books of the Bible and memorizing many important Bible dates, names and places. They also wrote reflection papers on formative sermons, world religions classes and books, such as: *The Master Plan Of Evangelism* (Coleman), *The Disciplined Life* (Taylor), *A Voice In The Wind* (Rivers), *Five Love Languages* (Chapman), *Tale Of Three Kings* (Edwards), *This Present Darkness* (Peretti), *Revolution Through Restoration I, II and III* (McKean), *Biblical Preaching* (Robinson, Second Edition), *A History Of The Spread Of Christianity In Modern Times* (Harding) at *KipMcKean.com* and many others!

They learned about practical ministry skills like preaching, Bible Talk leadership and writing. Along with these skills, they had to memorize the geographic map of the United States of America - states and their capitals - as well as all the countries of the world. To graduate, they had to attend 200 certified hours of Staff lessons and leadership conferences, 200 certified hours of Bible Talk Leaders Meetings, 200 certified hours of small group Bible discussions, and 200 certified hours of personal mentoring time. From one school in Los Angeles in 2012, we now have extension campuses in Boston, Lagos, Manila, Portland, Sao Paulo and Washington DC.

By spending time with one another, by walking with their Evangelist or Women's Ministry Leader as they are serving as Interns in the church and leading small groups, I believe that in every way the graduates of the ICCM Bachelor's Program are the best prepared in all of Christendom. Our goal is to make the ICCM as challenging of an experience as possible. We want the training to be tougher than the battle they will face leading churches later in life. Serving as President of ICCM-LA, along with my lovely wife Lianne, who serves as the Dean of Women, has been one of the greatest honors for me. It represents an incredible opportunity to train and build up presently about 70 amazing Interns who I know will do amazing things all over the world.

Let us examine some practicals of making leaders…

The first thing to consider is selection. ***"One of those days Jesus went out to a mountainside to pray, and spent the night praying to God. When morning came, He called His disciples to Him and chose twelve of them, whom He also designated Apostles…"*** (Luke 6:12-13) In "making leaders," it can be easy to start to think that those who like us or look up to us are doing well and growing. Of course, it is great to have close relationships; however, we are also looking for natural talents to strengthen, abilities to enhance, characters to craft, and skills to refine. Who we choose to work with will have long-term effects on our ministry! Like Jesus, we need to be very prayerful in selecting the people we will disciple. This should be similar to the way we would select a company in which we would invest a million dollars. It is that important.

Also, we must be careful not to only select leaders who are like us. ***"But in fact God has placed the parts in the body, every one of them, just as he wanted them to be. If they were all one part, where would the body be? As it is, there are many parts, but one body."*** (1 Corinthians 12:18-20) There are so many different character types and all of them are useful in ministry. Inflexible leaders surround themselves with only similar personalities to their own. This creates an xenophobic "ingroup" leadership which will not relate to the entire flock and will have dangerous flat-sides. This truly limits the potential of a ministry.

As we select leaders, what are some abilities that we should search for? Here are five:

1) They must lead charismatically. They must be people that others want to follow. (Mark 1:45; 2:1-2) We want to train leaders to call people to come and be with them. People do not just want what a leader can do for them; they want a leader who can walk with them. They want a relationship!

2) They must show a zeal for learning. Leaders must be able to learn new skills, languages, methods, etc. A leader is an expert at becoming an expert. (Proverbs 1:5) If a leader cannot learn and adapt, they will eventually be defeated by their challenges. "Leaders are readers!" We must read everything we can on the topic of leadership, organization and management.

3) They must be able to manage well. A leader must be able to manage time, money, people and resources. They must be able to create the desired outcome in their work. (1 Corinthians 14:40; Luke 16:11) A leader who cannot manage will never have the respect of particularly the older members, and his or her ministry will falter from lack of planning.

4) They must have command. Paul instructed the young Evangelist Titus, ***"These, then, are the things you should teach. Encourage and rebuke with all authority. Do not let anyone despise you."*** (Titus 2:15) A leader must have legitimate authority and develop an authoritative nature. When there is disunity in a ministry, it is often due to a lack of legitimacy, authority and

command of the leader. Command provides direction and unity. Without command, a leader is nothing more than a summer camp counselor who has bitten off more than he or she can chew. They must show the ability to wear the "tribal chief hat."

A ministry couple that has all five abilities listed above is Kolbe and Rebecca Gray!

5) They must be a hard worker. A leader must be able to pick up a shovel and dig a hole like an adult. As Thomas Edison once said, "Opportunity is missed by most because is it dressed in overalls and looks like work." Without the ability to work hard with determination, no one can serve as a leader in the Kingdom of God or see the amazing opportunities God puts before us. I expect the Interns that Lianne and I work with to show up with a Bible, notepad, up to date "to do list," calendar, laptop, pens, a camera and a recorder in their bag ready to get to work at every meeting. Does a plumber show up without their tools? I personally went into ministry

partially by making myself indispensable as the "photocopy boy," and "teen leader" of the Montreal International Church of Christ. As I proved my reliability opportunities came.

To elaborate a little further on the topic of work, ***"Since we live by the Spirit, let us keep in step with the Spirit."*** (Galatians 5:25) Hard work is impossible in ministry without keeping ***"in step"*** and having rhythm. One could go so far as to say that keeping your rhythm is one of the greatest factors in being an effective worker.

For example, when Lianne and I were living in London with a new born our rhythm was different than it is today. On the typical evening, Lianne would go to bed a little early at about 11pm and I would take care our first baby until about midnight when I would go to bed. Lianne would get up with Junior if he did not sleep through the night. At about 5:30am I would be back on duty with Junior and take him for my quiet time at a local café until about 8am. We would then have our family time until about 10:30am. In contrast to a normal 9 to 5 job, ministry happens in the evening so we found it best to connect as a family in the morning. After our family time, I would head to campus and Lianne would start her work day as well. I would come home around 10:30pm and we would repeat the process again. When David was born our rhythm changed, when the kids started school our rhythm changed, the rhythm changes in the summer when the kids are home or based on other needs in the ministry. Being adaptive and finding ways to put in long hours of work is imperative to ***"keep in step"*** with the Spirit and build a thriving ministry.

Before appointing a leader, especially as an Evangelist or Women's Ministry Leader, take the time to think and pray through these five abilities. This is not to say that a prospective leader will have these abilities and skills down pat. It is only to say that we must believe that they can achieve proficiency in them.

All this reminds me of Joe Willis, the diligent Sydney Church Evangelist, and his saying, "Evangelists are called to work on the church, not only in the church." A leader should not be running around getting everything done while others stand on the sidelines. Rather, a leader is someone who gets everyone growing, working and using their talents for the betterment of the church!

How do we build these skills into our prospective leaders? Where do we give them the opportunity to grow and experience the trials and errors necessary to become formidable leaders? All this is mere talk if we only do not practice. The answer is small groups! Using small groups to train and raise up leaders is not a new methodology. Let us look in the Old Testament and see what Moses' father-in-law thought of him single-handedly leading the "giant ameba" freshly emerged from the Red Sea - the people of Israel.

> *Moses' father-in-law replied [to Moses], "What you are doing is not good. You and these people who come to you will only wear yourselves out. The work is too heavy for you; you cannot handle it alone. Listen now to me and I will give you some advice, and may God be with you... But select capable men from all the people - men who fear God, trustworthy men who hate dishonest gain - and appoint them as officials over thousands, hundreds, fifties and tens. Have them serve as judges for the people at all times, but have them bring every difficult case to you; the simple cases they can decide themselves. That will make your load lighter, because they will share it with you. If you do this and God so commands, you will be able to stand the strain, and all these people will go home satisfied."*
> (Exodus 18:17-23)

In the words of Jethro, leading without small groups is *"not good,"* and *"God so commands!"* It is also a failure to imitate Jesus, which is also *"not good."* We must recognize and harness Jesus' and Jethro's methodology of small groups and use them to train a vast new generation of powerful and capable leaders. Let us take some time to consider this element of making leaders.

Not everyone who has worked at a high level of an organization can build and multiply small groups. As ministers, we need to keep our small group skills, our "guerrilla tactics," even as we grow and multiply. Our roots come from Jesus and the original small group, the Apostles. We must stay "guerrilla" and continue to hone our skills no matter how big our ministry becomes.

Bible Talks can be built in two ways. Firstly, they can be built from scratch. Secondly, we can split an effective Bible Talk in two. In the first case, we need to remember that things will "slow down" in the short term as new leaders are trained. This is because these leaders must learn to be effective in discipling, evangelism and working with one another. Just like figure skating, making small groups is much harder than it looks! A small group of disciples can take months to become truly unified, consistently mature and extremely effective. Enduring this initial period requires patience and convictions of steel, remembering that many small groups result in spectacular results… eventually!

While things slow down temporarily when we build Bible Talks from scratch the opposite is true when we break a Bible Talk that has become effective - or any effective ministry for that matter - in two. In that case we are taking effective leaders and putting them over a smaller group while giving other leaders - who they have raised up - a chance to lead. Just like when a mechanic puts a large engine into a smaller car, it becomes faster so when God puts more powerful leaders into a smaller ministry it gets more traction!

For example, in Los Angeles this year we realized that some of our Regions slowed down in growth as they crossed the 100-member threshold. The car had become too large for the engine! Even with everyone in Bible Talks there was just something about leading over 100 people that was challenging for one leadership couple serving in one "pulpit." A "pulpit" is a term used by my dear brother Raul Moreno, leader of the Sao Paulo ICC, and it refers to one group that meets almost every Sunday for worship. By breaking a Region into Sectors, we create new "pulpits." To address this slowdown in LA, we initiated "Project Wild Cat" which is a plan to break up our largest regions into smaller sectors of under 50 members each. This put some of our most talented leaders "back in the game" of advancing the church forcefully. For us in LA, the 100-person watershed seems to be the right time to "Sectorize" although this might be different for other churches.

At the Bible Talk level, in building a small group, we will need to ask disciples to invest in the group, to trust us, and thus to trust God. Achieving this "buy-in" is a requirement of building an effective small group. We cannot assume that everyone automatically understands what we are trying to do. Many people can be emotionally connected to an "assembly Christianity" model, not the small group model, without even knowing it. We need to take time to explain small groups to them and help them build convictions.

Also, remember that when people "buy in" or invest, they need to see results. We cannot sit idle even for a moment because ministry tempo is critical when building small groups. Proverbs 24:27 teaches us, *"Put your outdoor work in order and get your fields ready; after that, build your house."* We need to - hour by hour - cry out to God and work tirelessly to be fruitful and show results. Once we show results, we will be surprised at how much more people are willing to invest!

We also always need to remember that where there are no results, there is sin. We cannot go looking for worldly or humanistic solutions. Therefore, the right response to a lack of results is always a call to repentance. A lack of love for the lost, a lack of effort and a lack of sacrifice are some of the sins of omission that stop a group from being fruitful.

**The author and his wife enjoy time with freshly appointed
Bible Talk leaders in Chennai, India,
on the Bay of Bengal.**

At the same time as we are saddling our prospective leaders with small groups to lead, we must work hard to continue to earn the role of "coach" in their lives. People have faith that their coach wants the best for them and wants them to win. When that trust is there, "critique" is regarded as "help." On the other hand, when that relationship has not been built - or nourished - "critique" can be perceived as harshness.

Another consideration is that small group leadership is a three-dimensional subject. When considering how small groups make leaders, we must keep these three dimensions in mind. The first dimension is the traditional vertical perspective of leadership in which we join a small group, rise to leadership, and eventually lead many groups ourselves. This is the dimension with which most people are familiar. On the other hand, often overlooked is the second dimension; what I like to call the "depth of expertise" perspective. Micheal Williamson of London is a champion of this concept. I have learned from him that some people in our groups will grow their skills and become experts in their fields, as opposed to rising vertically. "Expert workers" can greatly improve the quality of the small groups we build, and this must be recognized. For example, perhaps someone may never oversee many small groups; however, as a singer they become expert songwriters and benefit the song ministry group in that way. We must honor the depth of capability and expertise of some people who, for whatever reason, may take longer to learn to lead other people. Creating a "vertical-only" leadership structure, by drawing attention only to those who lead others, can also force some people to lead others prematurely and result in trouble. That being said, all disciples should be stretched to serve in each and every capacity that they can.

The third dimension, another way to look at small groups, is the role-specific perspective: organizing small groups dedicated to specific needs, such as song ministry, Kids Kingdom, service to the poor, web ministry, administration, shepherding, ushers, etc. All these areas require small groups and small group leaders, and therefore, have the capacity to produce leadership.

It is always best to have specific Bible Talks for campus as Paul did in Acts 19:9, *"...some of them became obstinate; they refused to believe and publicly maligned the Way. So Paul left them. He took the disciples with Him and had discussions daily in the lecture hall of Tyrannus."* While we see here a Biblical example of campus Bible Talks, there is no direction from the Bible about creating exclusively "married" or "singles" Bible Talks. While not always possible, in general Lianne and I have always preferred to merge the marrieds and singles into "mingles" Bible Talks that have a geographic charge of a neighborhood or main street. Singles need marrieds to learn to hold down a job and get a spouse (if that is there calling), and the marrieds need the singles to prevent them from being isolated and estranged from the church.

This leads us to the question: Who is eligible to begin to lead a small group? Hebrews 5:11-14 teaches,

> **We have much to say about this, but it is hard to make it clear to you because you no longer try to understand. In fact, though by this time you ought to be teachers, you need someone to teach you the [First Principles] of God's Word all over again. You need milk, not solid food! Anyone who lives on milk, being still an infant, is not acquainted with the teaching about righteousness. But solid food is for the mature, who by constant use have trained themselves to distinguish good from evil.**

When disciples have spent time with us and learned to teach others, then it may be time to empower them with the responsibility of leading others. A **"mature"** disciple who is ready for leadership is not necessarily a certain age spiritually or physically but is someone who practices the **"First Principles"** consistently and who can teach others. This is the Biblical definition and the one we need to honor. When people are ready, then holding them back can embitter them. When they are not ready, then thrusting them into leadership can crush them. We are responsible for selecting the right people at the right time for the right job. Caleb Cohen, the powerful young leader of the South Region of the City of Angels ICC, once said, "God does not call you when you are ready to go. God calls you when you are ready to grow!"

As we make leaders, friction can sometimes arise between younger leaders and older leaders. (1 Samuel 17:28) Older leaders need to be persuaded to see that they have so much to offer, which includes leading, coaching as well as supporting. Concurrently, younger leaders must be taught to trust and seek input from more mature disciples. As the older and younger leaders become ***"perfectly united in mind and thought"*** (1 Corinthians 1:10), we can unlock enormous power in our ministries.

The mighty Challinors are the Coastal Cities Super Region Leaders of the City of Angels International Christian Church.

On campus, the goal is to have small groups led by campus students. The campus ministry is so essential to church growth that the church leader himself should be directly involved. He should be leading a small group until such point as he can be relieved by a young and very capable student leader or recent graduate. Leaving campus before finding a powerful replacement is a serious mistake with long-term consequences.

One might ask if successful small groups automatically become big groups. The goal of a small group is not "size" but multiplication. A successful small group germinates leadership and splits to become two small groups. Indeed, any group that has not generated new leadership and has not split into two needs to be carefully examined to ascertain what is wrong. In the words of John Causey, "You got to get smaller to get bigger!"

By building numerous small groups, we can convert an unlimited number of people and still care for each one. Every small group is like a mission team on its own that can meet the needs of its people and carry out the mission of Christ. The goal of multiplication of capable small groups must always be kept in mind!

Some might say, "Maybe so, but I have seen so many people burn out from leading small groups." Independent or abandoned small groups are not the methodology of Jesus. Rather, specially selected (2 Timothy 2:2) and carefully trained (Luke 6:40) disciples who are supervised (John 4:1-2) as they lead their small groups is Jesus' methodology. Jesus' methodology works, but only if we put His example into daily practice.

In this sense, Jesus' model of small groups follows a "teaching" model rather than the modern "sales team" model. Unfortunately, the sales team model can sometimes sneak into the church from the world. Christian leaders are not salesmen, and small groups are not sales teams. Jesus was referred to as "teacher" over eighty times in the New Testament, and His followers were referred to as "disciples" or students over two hundred and fifty. Salesmen burn out; teachers get "seasoned." This understanding flavors the way we lead our small groups and how we oversee others who lead them.

When leaders raise up and become mature in their abilities, they can replace us in the group and free us up to move on. This is a good thing - if they remain humble, coachable and obedient. Let them lead our group while we move on to build our next group! However, never leave a small group until we have replaced ourselves with a trained and loyal leader.

The sought-after Armor Bearer's and Shield Maiden's Pin is given to those Interns who complete a rigorous training program!

At the end of the day, small groups are the beating heart of church advancement. We cannot try to lead them all by ourselves! Bible Talks should be clustered together into "House Churches" with a House Church Leader Couple! House Churches should be organized into Sectors with a Sector Leader Couple. Sectors are organized into Regions and so forth. Clusters of Bible Talks led by a powerful Evangelist are what create the real momentum in any true Christian movement. Alexander Campbell had many wise words to share about church organization. He once said, "A church can do what an individual disciple cannot, and so can a district of churches do what a single congregation cannot."[6] This fact cannot be overstated.

Moving on from the concept of small groups, one of the other powerful things we can do to raise up leaders is not just preaching and working with them, but also resting with them! We should not rest from our people but rest with our people. Even in unwinding together, watching a movie, or sitting by the pool, we create memories and further "infect" them with the virus of leadership.

---

[6] *In Search of the Ancient Order* Vol. 1 page 156

Leaders, like all disciples, need to be "radicalized" and become "revolutionaries" who believe Jesus' plan for the world is the only plan that will work. This vision and conviction will keep leaders on track in times of hardship or temptation. (Matthew 17:13-17; Mark 10:41-45) Conversely, if we do not radicalize and nourish our leaders, then we are just creating a "house of cards" that will eventually fall. Keep the radical and the revolution in our ministry!

Another practical method is the "Safari." Sometimes as we are trying to inspire people to be leaders or to get back into the work of the ministry, it is good to "take them on Safari." That means bearing the brunt of the ministry work ourselves and bringing them in on critical moments, like the final studies of a conversion or having them disciple someone whom we have recently restored or baptized. They get to see the beauty of the "Safari" without the trouble of doing battle with the wild beasts and the elements. It can make them believe, once again, that God will reward us for our efforts. (Hebrews 11:6)

Let us close this chapter with this true story:

> *The wife of a man from the company of the prophets cried out to Elisha, "Your servant my husband is dead, and you know that he revered the Lord. But now his creditor is coming to take my two boys as his slaves."*
>
> *Elisha replied to her, "How can I help you? Tell me, what do you have in your house?"*
>
> *"Your servant has nothing there at all," she said, "except a small jar of olive oil."*

Elisha said, "Go around and ask all your neighbors for empty jars. Don't ask for just a few. Then go inside and shut the door behind you and your sons. Pour oil into all the jars, and as each is filled, put it to one side."

She left him and shut the door behind her and her sons. They brought the jars to her and she kept pouring. When all the jars were full, she said to her son, "Bring me another one."

But he replied, "There is not a jar left." Then the oil stopped flowing.

She went and told the man of God, and he said, "Go, sell the oil and pay your debts. You and your sons can live on what is left." (2 Kings 4:1-7)

This is a very moving and inspiring account of the remarkable widow who was blessed by God to provide for her family. It reminds me of the work of making leaders. Just like God did not give the widow more oil than she had jars for, God will not give us more additions to our ministry than we can lead. What if she had the need to put out twice as many jars? She would have received twice as much oil. What if we make twice as many leaders? God will give us twice as many members! We can limit our success if we do not call those we are training to dream of leading thousands, tens of thousands even millions. Jesus wants the whole world to be saved. (1 Timothy 2:4)

Making leaders is a huge slice of the pie of being a leader. It is how we expand the ministry, and it is how we evangelize the world in a generation. It is how churches survive and grow. Making leaders is about supervising specially selected (John 4:1-2) and carefully trained (Luke 6:40) disciples as they lead their small groups. Small groups are one of the most powerful tools to make seasoned leaders and to hone their abilities! If we do not have small groups, we need to build them so that we can imitate how Jesus raised up His leaders! Let us get this done and watch our ministries soar! Remember this, first came Jesus, then came the Apostles. First came the Apostles, then came the church. We simply cannot have more members than we can lead. Let us inspire and build up leaders and watch our ministries grow!

Camping out with some Interns (now Evangelists!) in 2016 - Mason Fetelika, Preston Inkley, the Author and Dennis Sloan.

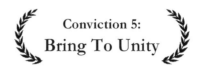

Conviction 5:
Bring To Unity

Unity makes the church an amazing place. Unity takes effort and work, but the results are worth it!

The author is the only white face in the unified Kinshasa International Christian Church in 2013.

Make every effort to keep the unity of the Spirit through the bond of peace. (Ephesians 4:3)

According to this Scripture, **"every effort"** must be made to keep **"the unity."** The Greek word for unity, henotēs, denotes unanimity and agreement. Whenever we are studying the Bible, we need to slip into the sandals of the first-century church and walk in their understanding of unity and not a modern interpretation. Scripture provides an example:

All the believers were one in heart and mind. No one claimed that any of his possessions was his own, but they shared everything they had. With great power the Apostles continued to testify to the resurrection of the Lord Jesus, and much grace was upon them all. There were no needy persons among them. For from time to time those who owned lands or houses sold them, brought the money from the sales and put it at the Apostles' feet, and it was distributed to anyone as he had need. (Acts 4:32-35)

This passage unlocks all kinds of secrets about how the first-century church lived. What is obvious is their incredible zeal; the trust they had for one another; and the sense of belonging they shared.

It is so important that we understand that the first-century church existed as a tribe within the greater Greco-Roman society. This society was based on "paterfamilias" or the concept of the "absolute rule of the father." In Greco-Roman society, a father had total legal authority over everyone in his household. It was a world based on large and powerful families, and almost everyone belonged to one for protection and sustenance. To this day Italian, Greek and Jewish families are still strong as a result. Obviously, a lot has changed since that time! The year A.D. 29, when Jesus died, was well before the "Enlightenment," "French Revolution," "Universal Sufferage," the "Industrial Revolution," "Feminism," "Darwins Theory of Evolution," "Class Struggle," "Philosophical Skepticism," "Relativism," "Humanism," and all of the major changes in popular thinking that have led to the modern highly individualistic Western society.

Even so, today hundreds of millions of people in the world still live and die in tribes much like those of the first-century disciples. It is extremely hard for the average Westerner, steeped in individualism, to grasp Acts 4:32-35 and the level of closeness and interdependence that the first-century church enjoyed. (More on this in Conviction 17: Join The Tribe.) In fact, for most Westerners, this concept of unity goes right over their heads.

**Our dear family, the Sirotkins and the Arnesons -
Russians, Ukrainians and Estonians - are
completely unified in Christ!**

Reflect on the following Scriptures: ***"But now in Christ Jesus you who once were far away have been brought near by the blood of Christ."*** (Ephesians 2:13) What was the basis of the unity of the church in contrast to the society around them? Was it their blood? Or their skin color? Or their lineage? ***"I speak to sensible people; judge for yourselves what I say. Is not the cup of thanksgiving for which we give thanks a participation in the blood of Christ? And is not the bread that we break a participation in the body of Christ? Because there is one loaf, we, who are many, are one body, for we all share the one loaf."*** (1 Corinthians 10:15-17) Disciples are unified by Jesus' blood and body and made into one family through it. We become sons and daughters of God and brothers and sisters of one another. ***"Consequently, you are no***

98

longer foreigners and strangers, but fellow citizens with God's people and also members of His household." (Ephesians 2:19)

The church of the first-century was a family and tribe, not an "ism," an ideological belief or a club to which one could merely subscribe. If we want to be unified with one another we must be unified in Christ. Any relationship that is not based on Christ will eventually be torn apart. The only way disciples will keep this in mind today is if we are constantly preaching it with power, just as the Apostles did.

The Bible describes the church as a loving, caring and supportive community. Although there were junctures at which that peace was disturbed, the ideal of unity is clearly prescribed. Infighting, distrust, discord, dissensions, factions and evil suspicions were always looked upon as sin and the trail signs of false teachers. Indeed, Jesus Himself prayed for unity among the believers and saw the unity of the church as one of the greatest tools of world evangelism:

> *My prayer is not for them alone. I pray also for those who will believe in me through their message, that all of them may be one, Father, just as you are in me and I am in you. May they also be in us so that the world may believe that you have sent me. I have given them the glory that you gave me, that they may be one as we are one - I in them and you in me - so that they may be brought to complete unity. Then the world will know that you sent me and have loved them even as you have loved me.* (John 17: 20-23)

An amazing part of this passage is how Jesus described the believers as needing to be *"BROUGHT to complete unity."* This presupposes that there will be disunity that will need to be addressed and rectified. There is no way to overemphasize that this is a major part of our work as leaders. If our group is not unified, then what are we baptizing people into? However, if a group is unified just as Christ commanded, then all things being equal, we can expect to have the same results that the first-century church had. Indeed, according to Jesus, if a group is unified as one, then the whole world will know that we are true disciples. (John 13:35) That would be incredible!

One of the greatest stories of Christian unity in our generation is the "The Portland Story." I had been baptized in the amazing Montreal International Church of Christ on June 21, 2001. I will be forever grateful to Ghislain Norman, Kolbe Anderson and the other brothers who helped to baptize me. It was incredible to be surrounded by fully committed disciples who were working together passionately to evangelize the world.

Unbeknownst to me, the disease of discord, dissent and contempt was spreading "cell to cell" in the Montreal Church and all the other ICOC churches around the world. Our fellowship of churches had expanded dramatically from one church in Boston in 1979 to almost 400 in 171 nations by 2001. God did so many amazing things and reached so many wonderful people through the ICOC Movement.

As a negative side effect of incredible growth, many of our church leaders lacked the training, experience and character to "sort out the shenanigans" (Chapter 3) that do inevitably come into every ministry. We did not regard bitterness and division with the seriousness that it should be taken. As the Lord says, *"They dress the wound of my people as though it were not serious. 'Peace, peace,' they say, when there is no peace."* (Jeremiah 6:14) Also, our membership lacked the Biblical understanding to address grievances and contentious issues in a mature manner. As the Bible says, *"...the Lord's servant must not be quarrelsome but must be kind to everyone, able to teach, not resentful."* (2 Timothy

2:24) Because of these failures, God handed us over to open rebellion in 2003, and we descended into a dark abyss of chaos.

False teachers rose at that time, and instead of teaching Biblical unity, they preached rage and judgment. They instigated rebellion and had become unaccountable "kings" over their own newly independent and wealthy kingdoms. While the initial outbursts of this insurrection were, perhaps spontaneous, it quickly became a manufactured rebellion. So many suffered so much during the fall of the ICOC and only a small handful benefited and continue to benefit from this tragedy to this day. They preside over wealthy independent churches with no oversight or accountability, while their members suffer from the lack of unity, the lack of direction, and consequently, the lack joy that comes from being used by God to have abundant fruit. All the things that come with a central leadership and a central leader.

The "new vision" for the church, put forward by these false teachers, was consensus leadership - with no one clear leader - and a canceling of all structure, including discipling relationships and Bible Talks. A message of "cheap grace" with no expectations was ushered in like a golden calf (Exodus 32:1-6), and the dream of evangelizing the world in a generation was called "false teaching" and "impossible." The doctrine of autonomy meant every church went in its own direction. In the wake autonomy, divorces multiplied, droves fell away, and thousands upon thousands were left shipwrecked in their faith. Before my very eyes, I saw members of the church tear one another apart as only Satan could orchestrate.

With all this tragedy and darkness, a small light began to shine very brightly! The ravaged Portland Church was the place where God carried Kip and Elena McKean when everything came crashing down. Under their godly leadership, a church of about 25 disciples in July 2003 became fully committed and multiplied to 120 sold-out

> *"Under their godly leadership, a church of about 25 disciples in July 2003 became fully committed and multiplied to 120 sold-out disciples..."*

disciples by January 2004! Instead of backpedaling on the convictions of the first-century church, Kip and Elena preached God's Word and that light became visible to many around the world.

Instead of having open forums to vent anger and rage, they unified the church with a "Night of Atonement," in which disciples could share their own sins and shortcomings. Instead of canceling all structure, they made sure that every disciple had a discipling partner and that no one was left alone. Instead of tearing down leadership, they appointed numerous Bible Talk Leaders, Deacons, Evangelists, CyberEvangelists, and Elders-in-Training. Instead of preaching cheap grace and trying to win a popularity contest, they became great among us by their service and humility. (Matthew 23:11)

I will never forget how the Spirit guided me to meet with Kip in Portland in 2004 at the First International Discipleship Jubilee entitled, "The Lord Of The Fellowship." I had attempted to reach out to other church leaders in what was left of the ICOC, and after receiving no response, let alone direction, Lianne and I reached out to Kip and Elena in Portland, as it was already the fastest growing church in the ICOC in 2004. I was amazed that Kip put his number on the website, and when I called and left a message, Kip phoned me right back a few hours later! He invited Lianne and I to the Jubilee, and the church graciously and warmly welcomed us as family.

On the first day of the conference, Kip met with me at 7 a.m. at Starbucks beside the Ambridge Event Center. That morning at

Starbucks, immediately following my first sip of Verona, Kip opened the Scriptures with me and shared his clear and unapologetic vision. It was so good to "hear and feel" Kip's faith to gather the remnant, his zeal to evangelize the nations, and his passion for God's honor. Through that talk and Kip's lesson at the conference - "A Great Light Has Dawned" - I was heartbroken to realize that most in the ICOC, including myself, had abandoned living the life of a disciple. Likewise, I was so convicted that I had passively chosen to abandon the Lord's call to evangelize the nations in our generation. (1 Timothy 2:3-4)

After Kip's lesson, I saw that the solutions were not complicated: I needed to return to God with all my heart; call all others to do the same; and then be willing to withstand the "persecution" that would surely come. Most frightening to me was the threat of "disfellowshipment" - the ungodly severing of relationships from all those who meant so much to Lianne and I. Jesus addressed the same threat for those who would follow Him in the first century, *"All this I have told you so that you will not go astray. They will put out of the synagogue; in fact, a time is coming when anyone who kills you will think he is offering a service to God. They will do such things because they have not known the Father or me."* (John 16:1-2)

That night, at the evening session of the Jubilee as we all sang together, my spiritual amnesia about God's desire for a glorious church quickly dissipated, as the *"new wine"* of a "sold-out commitment" once again began to flow through my veins. *"And no one puts new wine into old wineskins. For the wine will burst the wineskins, and the wine and the skins would both be lost. New wine calls for new wineskins."* (Mark 2:22)

Lianne and I were so excited to embrace once again the Biblical truths that we had learned as younger disciples! After the Portland

Jubilee, I returned to Canada with the hope of bringing revival to my cherished Montreal Church. To my excitement, the leadership of the church received the *"new wine"* with joy at first and joined the new movement now called the "Portland Movement" and later the "SoldOut Movement." However, as tensions mounted between the few that wanted to be "sold-out" and the many that embraced the broad path of lukewarmness, I came to see what a tough fight this was going to be. This situation played out all over the world, as disciples were persecuted by many in what was left of the ICOC for wanting to return to committed discipleship. Again, Jesus was so right that when *"new wine"* is put into *"old wineskins"* (traditional churches), *"the wine [will] burst the wineskins, and the wine and the skins [will] both be lost."* So as not to *"be lost,"* Lianne and I fled for our spiritual lives to Toronto to begin a church of only sold-out disciples - *"new wine calls for new wineskins."* We had the right idea, but I was not trained.

After the Montreal Church severed ties with the God's new Movement in 2006, Lianne and I began to gather the Toronto Remnant Group. In a year's time, despite my inexperience, God grew our church from just the two of us to 17 members! In May of 2007, Lianne and I were asked to be the 41st and 42nd members of the Los Angeles Mission Team launched from the Portland Church.

What an education to watch master builders - Kip and Elena - construct the mighty City of Angels International Christian Church from scratch! On a side note, in 2008, the Portland Church - like the Montreal Church - gave into fear and deserted the new movement departing back to the "safety" of lukewarmness. Consequently, these 42 were the distillation and fermentation of the *"new wine"* of what was called the SoldOut Movement! As of today, the Spirit has taken "us" in just ten years from that one congregation of 42 to become over 5,000 disciples in 76 churches in 32 nations on all six populated continents of the world!

On the other hand, now even top ICOC leaders have admitted that the ICOC is dead as a movement. A prominent ICOC leader and one of the architects of autonomy, Gordon Ferguson, recently wrote, "[At the end of 2015, the ICOC] have 667 congregations overall 381 of which baptized between 1 and 10 people, and 122 had zero baptisms. Thus [in 2015], of our 667 churches, 503 (75%) baptized between 0 and 10 people in a year's time. And let me state the obvious here - when seventy-five percent of our congregations are baptizing between zero and ten people per year, things are not close to going well." [7] While this statement is true, sadly, Mr. Ferguson and others who have guided the ICOC these past 15 years have yet to claim any responsibility. My purpose in quoting Mr. Ferguson here is to clearly show the difference between groups that value unity - only attainable through centralized leadership and a central leader - and those that do not. The contrast could not be more stark.

Over the course of 13 short years since that day at the Starbucks at the Ambridge Event Center, my life has been completely changed many times over. I marvel at the incredible power of God - as He has *"brought to unity"* disciples from every walk of life, every continent and every race. The light that is beaming in the darkness is reaching more and more souls!

Let us now walk through some basics and practicals of this principle. One of the first major obstacles that we face as leaders trying to bring unity to our group is building trust. In the world of theory, Christians know that they need to be part of a unified group for many reasons. However, when they belong to such a group - composed of imperfect people with imperfect leaders - they find that distrust can become a powerful barrier to unity. When there is distrust in a group, people tend to break into factions by race, primary language,

---

[7] G. Furguson, (2016) *My Three Lives*, Page 127

profession or even tax bracket, instead of being unified across these barriers by the blood of Christ. (Ephesians 2:14-18)

When we are facing persistent issues of distrust, it is not sufficient to set about to "earn" the trust of our group; nor is it wise to teach the group that they have to "earn" the trust of one another. Biblically, trust must be given up front. Sinners who will inevitably make mistakes cannot earn trust. Teaching "the earning of trust" simply sets the group up for disappointments and resentment. Instead, we need to instill the Biblical definition of trust into the group: Love *"...always protects, always trusts, always hopes, always perseveres. Love never fails."* (1 Corinthians 13:7-8) We *"always trust"* because we are commanded to love. (John 13:34) Leaders need to live with imperfect members and prepare them patiently for works of service. (Ephesians 4:12) Members must learn to trust their imperfect leaders. Even when mistakes are made and disciples wound one another, we *"do not repay evil with evil or insult with insult, but with blessing, because to this [we are] called so that [we] may inherit a blessing."* (1 Peter 3:9)

So many things can cause disunity. Disunity can come from differences in doctrine on debatable matters (Romans 9:14), from character differences (1 Corinthians 12:12-26), from differences of opinion on goals and direction in the ministry (Hebrews 13:17), or cultural or racial differences. (Galatians 3:28) Regardless of the reason, differences need to be brought to terms and set at the foot of the cross. In 1 Corinthians 1:10, Paul states, *"I appeal to you, brothers and sisters, in the name of our Lord Jesus Christ, that all of you agree with one another in what you say and that there be no divisions among you, but that you be perfectly united in mind and thought."* This is the radical standard of the Bible, and no one has the right to water it down or change it!

Building unity is also about creating a powerful sense of belonging and identity. This cannot be overstated. For lack of a better word, we need to make our groups "COOL!" This "esprit de corps," or spirit of belonging, is an intangible quality that comes when disciples realize who they are and of what they are part!

"When morning came, He called His disciples to Him and chose twelve of them, whom He also designated Apostles..." (Luke 6:13) Jesus could have called His group anything, but He chose them and gave them an inspiring name and purpose: Apostles or "Messengers!" Jesus defined the membership of His group and gave them a purpose. These are very important ingredients to building a powerful and unified ministry.

The author gathered the leadership of the Western United States and Canada World Sector at the Latin America Missions Conference in Mexico City, Mexico in February 2017.

Peter said, *"But you are a chosen people, a royal priesthood, a holy nation, God's special possession, that you may declare the praises of Him who called you out of darkness into His wonderful light."* (1 Peter 2:9) So many cool names in one verse and what an amazing purpose! It is a sin to fail to build an inspiring identity into our ministries. We cannot make our group just another "meeting"; we need to make them a defined "cool" team with a purpose!

When disciples feel unified with those around them and are building the best friendships of their lives, the love they develop for one another allows them to overlook many faults that we may have as leaders. As Peter writes in 1 Peter 4:8, *"Above all, love each other deeply, because love covers over a multitude of sins."* Raul Moreno has a great quote which I believe to be totally true, "The way you love people is the way you love God." Disciples must be known for our great friendships!

By preaching that the blood of Christ unites us, by training in trust, by skillfully navigating through debatable matters, by building an indestructible membership, by making our groups "cool" - with both identity and purpose - and by appreciating the benefits of unity, leaders can build a unity that will last. It takes pleading with God for wisdom to become the experts in this field that we need to be.

In every way, I pray that your ministries are forever happy and unified. Never that forget the consequences of disunity are too severe and the benefits too awesome for us to fail to put everything we have into making our churches a place of belonging, healing, vision and love. Let us take hold of the dream of a spotless church - unified in Christ - and forcefully advance this vision to make it a daily reality.

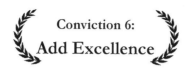

Conviction 6:
Add Excellence

Excellence makes all the difference between success and failure. Quality and excellence can compensate for a lack in other areas.

The Kernans, upon being appointed the City of Angels ICC Leaders, presented the McKeans with a world map of the Crown of Thorns Project.

Finally, brothers, whatever is true, whatever is noble, whatever is right, whatever is pure, whatever is lovely, whatever is admirable - if anything is excellent or praiseworthy - think about such things. (Philippians 4:8)

Excellence... the final frontier. Paul writes the stirring words of the Scripture above to the church at Philippi. Philippi was a town founded by Philip of Macedon, who was the father of Alexander the Great. The city was founded to protect key strategic roads and gold mines from raiders and marauding bandits. Later, Emperor Augustus made Philippi into a famous Roman Army pensioners' colony. When Paul writes to the converts there, he urges them to think about excellent things. In a town founded by such disciplined people, I am sure they did not have far to look! Excellence was a trademark of the Romans and Greeks who founded this remarkable town.

Today, as in antiquity, excellence guards the gold and the route to it from the undeserving. The ranks of the fruitless and unfulfilled are packed with highly intelligent, passionate and charismatic people with amazing dreams. However, as the Scripture says, *"He who works his land will have abundant food, but he who chases fantasies lacks judgment."* (Proverbs 12:11) It is often the ungifted few - who value excellence - who end up owning the gold.

"Even if we lack talent or resources, hard work and dedication to excellence can make up what is lacking."

When Paul was addressing the Corinthian Church, he wrote in 2 Corinthians 8:7, *"But just as you excel in everything - in faith, in speech, in knowledge, in complete earnestness and in your love for us - see that you also excel in this grace of giving."* The disciples in the Kingdom of God are supposed to value excellence and be excellent in everything they do. Even if we lack talent or resources, hard work and dedication to excellence can make up what is lacking. Excellence must be expected in the Kingdom.

In 1 Corinthians 14:12, the Bible commands, *"So it is with you. Since you are eager to have spiritual gifts, try to excel in gifts that build up the church."* It is not just the gifts themselves that build up the church - it is excellence in those gifts that build up the church! Too many great disciples waste their gifts by failing to become excellent in them.

Excellence requires self-denial and perseverance. People who value excellence work hard to achieve it. Those who value excellence are always interested in quality and refinement. They repeat the same task over and over to get it right. They are concerned about the details, the small things, the final polishes and this care always pays off.

The areas that I have failed in personally are excellence in scheduling time to exercise enough and eat in a balanced and healthy way. Ever since I was married - and no longer working out four times a week at university - I have gained and held on to my weight. This is a serious shortcoming. It would seem simple, eat less, exercise more however a lack of deep conviction, other priorities and a lack of consistency made weight loss elusive. However, through seeking input from Jee Blackwell and Michele Williamson (both serious fitness gurus) I have now been doing intermittent fasting, disciplined diet and four workouts a week for several months now and have lost 25 pounds. I still have about 35 to go, so my prayer is that I stay disciplined and focused on excellence when it comes to my health.

In general, a lack of excellence comes from trying to get by on talent alone without dedication or discipline. Sometimes those who lack excellence are obligated to work very hard at the last minute to just meet the minimum standards. But there are no "minimum standards" in the Kingdom of God. God tests the quality of everyone's work.

By the grace God has given me, I laid a foundation as a wise builder, and someone else is building on it. But each one should build with care. For no one can lay any foundation other than the one already laid, which is Jesus Christ. If anyone builds on this foundation using gold, silver, costly stones, wood, hay or straw, their work will be shown for what it is, because the Day will bring it to light. It will be revealed with fire, and the fire will test the quality of each person's work. If what has been built survives, the builder will receive a reward. If it is burned up, the builder will suffer loss but yet will be saved - even though only as one escaping through the flames. (1 Corinthians 3:10-13)

Ministry is all about using what we have and building with quality. That is the "whole ball game." Careful attention to excellence can bring home the victory when the fire comes. Excellence can trump so many disadvantages and is an absolute must for any ministry. Excellence can make up for a lack of training, money, talent and numbers and in fact can produce all these things.

Conversely, mediocrity brings so much liability to every enterprise. Never give in to the narcotic of mediocrity. In the darkest hours believe in God, say no to the sloppiness, irresponsibility and dereliction that hopelessness brings.

I will never forget attending my first Global Leadership Conference (GLC) in 2009 whose them was "Go Into All The World!" The GLC is an amazing conference held annually somewhere around the world. This year it is in Manila, Philippines! My first GLC was a "magical," spiritual event with so many incredible speakers and disciples from all over the world - a unique event with a true sense of purpose. I have attended these conferences for the past seven years, and they have been so instrumental in my spiritual growth.

One cannot imagine how humbled I felt when I was asked to serve as Director of the GLC. I felt a major responsibility to make sure the conference was as impactful for others as it had been for me in years past. I had already run three international conferences in London, England, entitled "The Gathering," but the GLC was something truly global.

I had no idea how much I would grow from organizing this momentous event. The lessons I have learned have had an impact on almost every other area of my ministry and my life. It has fundamentally changed my character.

The 2013 Global Leadership Conference - "Prophets And Kings" - was the first conference directed by the author.

Every year, we spend months planning the conference with some of the most talented leaders in the CAICC. Those who have served nobly on my GLC Staff include Susan Bond, LuJack Martinez, Chris Adams, Ricky and Coleen Challinor, Emilio and Tatiana Bonilla, Heidi Santa Cruz, Ryan and Iyonna Keenan, Nick and Jacque Economo, Jake Studer, Jared McGee, Krystal Legarda, Megan

Mathews, Yelena Astanin, Jose Otero, Tyler and Shay Sears, Evan and Kelly Bartholomew, Curtis and Morgan Valdez, Rob Onekea, Damon James, Rebecca Rico, Luke and Brandyn Speckman, Mike Purdy, Lance Underhill, Karen Maciel and Joel Parlour. We all work together for weeks to develop the conference plan. We pour over the singing, the program, the themes, the merchandise, the coordination, the transportation, the food, the budget, the videos, the design, the logos, the registration, the photography and the lodging for delegates - every detail!

At Christmas in 2012 in New York City, the Kernan family visited Dr. Andrew and Patrique Smellie, who were leading the New York City ICC. The Smellies are a couple who exemplify excellence.

After all the grand strokes of planning are complete, I then take the program and the whole plan to our dear brother Kip, who then takes over thirty hours (in long meetings with me) to refine, correct and develop almost every detail of the conference plan. Kip adds not only a refinement, but a grace, a "classiness," a sense of pageantry and a masterful finishing touch to this very special, once-a-year event. The first year, there were thousands of errors, typos, mistakes and shortcomings to work through to get the conference to a polished level of excellence. The second year, there was probably just under a thousand things to work through that needed his attention. Last year, I was in the hundreds. This year, God willing, we will be in the dozens! I can genuinely say that I now have a much deeper conviction about excellence and I have seen the difference it can make. It has taken hundreds of hours of discipling to ingrain excellence into my urban Irish thinking.

I am extremely grateful to Kip for investing his time (which was probably been excruciatingly painful for him) to turn a rash, "shoot from the hip" Evangelist into someone who could run a world-class, spiritual leadership event. The GLC has changed me forever.

Through discipling and teaching one another, we must, with love and patience, bring everyone in our ministry to value and pursue excellence. In Colossians 1:28, the Bible teaches, *"We proclaim Him, admonishing and teaching everyone with all wisdom, so that we may present everyone perfect in Christ."* Bringing people closer to Jesus through teaching His Word and through His power is an amazing way to show love for those under our care, by helping them to become like Jesus - excellent in all things.

Excellence has its place in every one of our ministries. *"Then this Daniel became distinguished above all the other presidents and satraps, because an excellent spirit was in him. And the king planned to set him over the whole kingdom."* (Daniel 6:3) By instilling excellence in the campus ministry especially, in every aspect of a campus student's life, we can eventually thread excellence through the whole church. Imagine if every campus student was brought to a standard of excellence during college, and then, upon graduation, entered the singles or marrieds ministry of the church with that deep conviction in their hearts. Imagine that they begin their professional careers demanding from themselves that same standard of excellence they were called to in their college years. What a service that would be to them, to their respective places of employment, to the church and to everyone they will encounter for the rest of their lives!

In Los Angeles in July 2016, we spent the month to raise the quality and excellence of our ministry as a whole. We called it the "Prepared for Service Project." In the course of the month, we conducted a "Night of Atonement" in every Region - where men and women came together in small groups to confess their sins to one another. (Proverbs 28:13) Following that, every Region Leader Couple, along with their Shepherding Couples, took the time to meet with the most vulnerable members for "life talks" to encourage and minister to them. This set us up to revisit the whole discipling and mentoring "tree" and make sure that we were having excellent and quality weekly discipling times across the whole congregation. We then had regional "Bible Talk Expos," where each Bible Talk stood before the church and shared their Bible Talk name, members, geographic territory and goals for the year! This radically invigorated the whole congregation.

In eager expectation, we then conducted a "Worship Service Devotional" to review every part of our worship services. We taught about singing, prayer, what the welcome should look like, what the communion should be like, etc. Because of this, we experienced a massive jump in the quality and excellence of our worship services! Pageantry, ceremony, timely and smart services are so important to model excellence and seed it into the whole church.

This prepared us for our "Bring Your Neighbor Day" (BYND) and "Men's Forum!" On our BYND and Men's Forum, many regions broke attendance records, as they ushered their friends and family into a church that was prepared, organized, excellent and eager to greet them! Two weeks after the BYND, we had a powerful Harvest Sunday capping off a harvest month, which was the most fruitful the church had ever had - 48 baptisms! By applying excellence and concern for quality to all aspects of our ministry, the CAICC became a stronger and more potent instrument for God to use. This took quite a bit of energy and effort, but remember this, "More sweat now, less blood later."

Since excellence is a command of God and if we have convictions about what it can do to help build our ministry, then what is holding us back? What are some areas in which we can become more excellent? Cleanliness, punctuality and completing tasks carefully and thoroughly are all trademarks of an excellent leader. What can we do to improve our ministry? Do we preach on excellence? Are our services and meetings excellent? Does your ministry need a "Prepared for Service" overhaul? Imagine all that can be accomplished if we add excellence to all the amazing talents we already possess. For the honor and glory of God, I plead with you to take everything we already have working for us in the ministry, and add excellence!

We have our few; we have our miracles and we have combed through our entire ministry - Bible Talk by Bible Talk - to call everyone to be "sold out" for Jesus. Our leaders are abounding; our group is unified; our work is excellent. Let us move on to the next set of convictions.

The next four convictions will stretch and pull our ministries in new directions. These tools give us new ways to think about ministry. This vital section of the book is about expanding. We will learn to expand into places with which we may not be familiar. We will learn to expand the message to people whom we may have never fully understood. We will learn to expand our message to the Internet and watch our ministries grow!

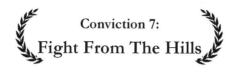

Conviction 7:
Fight From The Hills

As disciples, we do not fight only for territory; we fight for souls. What are the hills and plains that God wants us to liberate for Him?

The City of Angels International Christian Church Staff on top of Mount Shalom (Mount Hollywood) in 2016 praying for our Bring Your Neighbor Day!

[Jesus] went to Nazareth, where He had been brought up, and on the Sabbath day He went into the synagogue, as was His custom. He stood up to read, and the scroll of the prophet Isaiah was handed to Him. Unrolling it, He found the place where it is written:

'The Spirit of the Lord is on me,
because He has anointed me

119

to proclaim good news to the poor.
He has sent me to proclaim freedom for the prisoners
and recovery of sight for the blind,
to set the oppressed free,
to proclaim the year of the Lord's favor.'

Then He rolled up the scroll, gave it back to the attendant and sat down. The eyes of everyone in the synagogue were fastened on Him... (Luke 4:16-20 Abridged)

This is a revolutionary Scripture that is the beating heart of any true church and ministry. Jesus had great compassion, as should we, for the spiritually poor, those imprisoned in sin, blind to their spiritual reality, and under the oppression of evil in their lives. This gets the blood of every disciple pumping and makes us want to go out and share our faith with the lost!

Was Jesus saying that He had come to "preach to the poor" because He was a nice guy? Was He just a "bleeding heart," or did Jesus have a strategy to conquer the world? (Acts 1:8) We do believe Jesus was a "nice guy," of course, in that He was kind; however, He was not sentimental. Everything Jesus did was part of an intentional and deliberate plan to liberate mankind.

To their shame, the religious leaders of His day looked down on Jesus' passion for the poor and the downtrodden. Jesus rebuked them saying, **"'Truly I tell you, the tax collectors and the prostitutes are entering the Kingdom of God ahead of you. For John came to you to show you the way of righteousness, and you did not believe him, but the tax collectors and the prostitutes did. And even after you saw this, you did not repent and believe him.'"** (Matthew 21:31-32) Jesus was adamant and determined to engage those in the "gutter" of society and could always defend His plan!

Again, in Mark 2:16-17, Jesus interacts with the religious leaders on this topic, **"When the teachers of the law who were Pharisees saw Him eating with the sinners and tax collectors, they asked His disciples: 'Why does He eat with tax collectors and sinners?' On hearing this, Jesus said to them, 'It is not the healthy who need a doctor, but the sick. I have not come to call the righteous, but sinners.'"** Once more, we see that Jesus was not just accidentally hanging out with some "derelicts" from the block. Jesus had a methodology and was sticking with it.

Interestingly, Jesus started His ministry in the countryside, and some of His first disciples were fishermen. It is hard to say if they would have even been literate. Not only was He focused on the poor and oppressed, but He soon sent His disciples village to village, giving richly to the spiritually destitute, liberating the imprisoned, and healing the ill. (Matthew 10:5-6, 23) Even though the countryside was not "decisive ground," as perhaps Jerusalem was, it provided an open environment for His message and a place where He could train His disciples to multiply.

Jesus believed that anyone could change. As the car dealership slogan goes, "We buy lemons!" He would not turn away anyone who truly wanted to be a disciple. Jesus believed in this approach to people and believed that with some good old-fashioned discipling and love, they would become incredible instruments in God's hands.

I remember Kip showing me the following poem for the first time. I was struggling to have a vision for an older "remnant" brother who had "let me down" on several occasions. It is now my favorite poem and reminds me of the vision we need to have for every person.

The Touch Of The Masters Hand - The Old Violin
by Myra Welch

'Twas battered and scarred,
And the auctioneer thought it
hardly worth his while
To waste his time on the old violin,
but he held it up with a smile.
"What am I bid, good people," he cried,
"Who starts the bidding for me?"
"One dollar, one dollar, do I hear two?"
"Two dollars, who makes it three?"
"Three dollars once, three dollars twice, going for three,"
But, no, from the room far back a gray bearded man
Came forward and picked up the bow,
Then wiping the dust from the old violin
And tightening up the strings,
He played a melody, pure and sweet
As sweet as the angel sings.
The music ceased and the auctioneer
With a voice that was quiet and low,
Said, "What now am I bid for this old violin?"
As he held it aloft with its bow.
"One thousand, one thousand, do I hear two?"
"Two thousand, who makes it three?"
"Three thousand once, three thousand twice,
Going and gone," said he.
The audience cheered,
But some of them cried,
"We just don't understand."
"What changed its worth?"
Swift came the reply.
"The touch of the Master's hand."

And many a man with life out of tune
All battered and bruised with hardship
Is auctioned cheap to a thoughtless crowd
Much like that old violin.
A mess of pottage, a glass of wine,
A game and he travels on.
He is going once, he is going twice,
He is going and almost gone.
But the Master comes,
And the foolish crowd never can quite understand,
The worth of a soul and the change that is wrought
By the touch of the Master's hand.

No one is born in this world for whom Jesus did not die on the cross. We need to strive to help everyone to be like this "old" violin. Most churches have deep convictions about seeking and saving the broken. In the City of Angels Church in 2016, we initiated "Project Heart Language," which is an effort to build powerful "second language" devotionals. These devotionals, now in Spanish and Tagalog, have allowed us to reach many recently migrated immigrants who do not yet speak English very well. In Los Angeles, about 31% of the population do not speak English as a first language. By growing these devotionals and multiplying the number of languages we can have them in, we believe we will liberate poor and disadvantaged of Los Angeles - the immigrant community who seek a better life for their children in America.

However, while seeking the downtrodden, we must not lose the heart to save everyone! We must go after the "prize," which is all mankind! Jesus' heart was not only for the oppressed but also for Jerusalem, which was the Los Angeles of their world!

"Jerusalem, Jerusalem, you who kill the prophets and stone those sent to you, how often I have longed to gather your

children together, as a hen gathers her chicks under her wings, and you were not willing." (Luke 13:34-35) It was always on Jesus' heart to build a thriving ministry in Jerusalem, and He periodically brought His disciples there. (Mark 10:32) This is where a lot of ministries fail. They do not have the ambition to take on the tough areas and top campuses!

Perhaps the greatest vindication of Jesus' ministry to the poor, imprisoned, blind and oppressed, to the backward villages surrounding Jerusalem, came from the High Priest when he said to the Apostles: *"'We gave you strict orders not to teach in this name,' he said. 'Yet you have filled Jerusalem with your teaching and are determined to make us guilty of this man's blood.'"* (Acts 5:28) Here we see that a single man walking by the Sea of Galilee (Mark 1:14), the greatest revolutionary of all time, had successfully filled Jerusalem with His message!

He had done so by first fighting for the impoverished and sinful hearts of uneducated men (Acts 4:13), the poor and the oppressed. (Matthew 21: 31-32) Then not satisfied until He conquered the whole land, He trained those men and women to fill Jerusalem with His teaching! Jesus was victorious not only in the village, but also the city and the temple courts! Jesus proved not only to be kind… but a genius!

Jesus had a strategy to break into Jerusalem and have a powerful impact there. That strategy relied on investing heavily in the poor and disenfranchised. We see His successful approach continued to prove itself, as not only the destitute were converted after His death and resurrection, but also the elite, *"So the Word of God spread. The number of disciples in Jerusalem increased rapidly, and a large number of priests became obedient to the faith."* (Acts 6:7)

As a testimony to how deeply Jesus had embedded His convictions, the Apostles were the only ones to stay in Jerusalem when the persecution hit in Acts 8:1. The Apostles had become immovable fixtures of Jerusalem and were deeply entrenched. Their final testimony was their martyrdom for the cause.

In all likelihood, like most ministries, we can find ourselves to be already among the underprivileged! We are already among the "sinners" and deprived, and it is time to have ambition for the whole land and all the people as Jesus did!

The conquest of the Promised Land foreshadowed the conquest of world evangelism. Study this Scripture:

> *The men of Judah went down to fight against the Canaanites living in the hill country, the Negev and the western foothills. They advanced against the Canaanites living in Hebron (formerly called Kiriath Arba) and defeated Sheshai, Ahiman and Talmai. From there they advanced against the people living in Debir (formerly called Kiriath Sepher)... The Lord was with the men of Judah. They took possession of the hill country but they were unable to drive the people from the plains, because they had chariots fitted with iron...* (Judges 1:8-19 Abridged)

The men of Judah fought a grueling war in the hill country over a period of years, taking strongholds one after the other. They fought in small bands united by family and with a hunger to conquer the Promised Land. Sadly, after conquering the hills, they failed to pour down into the plains to finish the conquest. God was not pleased that the whole land was not conquered.

The Angel of the Lord went up from Gilgal to Bokim and said, "I brought you up out of Egypt and led you into the land I swore to give to your ancestors. I said, 'I will never break my covenant with you, and you shall not make a covenant with the people of this land, but you shall break down their altars.' Yet you have disobeyed me. Why have you done this? And I have also said, 'I will not drive them out before you; they will become traps for you, and their gods will become snares to you."

When the Angel of the Lord had spoken these things to all the Israelites, the people wept aloud, and they called that place Bokim. There they offered sacrifices to the Lord. (Judges 2:2-5)

The Bible states, ***"For everything that was written in the past was written to teach us, so that through the endurance taught in the Scriptures and the encouragement they provide we might have hope."*** (Romans 15:4) Therefore, we must believe that the Scriptures are trying to teach us something through the struggle of the men of Judah during the very critical conquest of the Promised Land.

The Israelites had mixed success as too many of our ministries do! They took the *"hill country,"* but failed to descend into the fertile plains and conquer the whole land. On the plains, the Canaanites were wealthier and better equipped with iron chariots. Plains warfare happens when both sides seek decisive victory at one time and place. Biblically, the result of battle on the plains is bloody and quick. (1 Samuel 17: 51-53) The Israelites preferred to use the terrain to their advantage and fight where the enemy could not bring their iron chariots and massive armies to bear. They wanted to deny the Canaanites decisive battle and wear them down instead. It was

126

certainly not beyond God's power to give them the plains, but in their lack of faith, they chose not to conquer it! After God had rebuked the men of Judah, they sacrificed to the Lord... but still refused to go down into the plains!

Some great movies to watch to understand this concept are *Red Dawn* (both the 1984 original and remake), *The Patriot*, *The Battle Of Algiers*, *Michael Collins*, *The Wind That Shakes The Barley*, *Charlie Wilson's War*, *Black Hawk Down*, *Che*, *The Battle Of Haditha* and *Platoon*. I have personally found these movies motivating while on small mission teams.

Why was God so upset that they only conquered the hills? Study this Scripture:

> **After the death of Moses the servant of the Lord, the Lord said to Joshua son of Nun, Moses' aide: "Moses my servant is dead. Now then, you and all these people, get ready to cross the Jordan River into the land I am about to give to them - to the Israelites. I will give you every place where you set your foot, as I promised Moses. Your territory will extend from the desert to Lebanon, and from the great river, the Euphrates - all the Hittite country - to the Mediterranean Sea in the west. No one will be able to stand against you all the days of your life. As I was with Moses, so I will be with you; I will never leave you nor forsake you. Be strong and courageous, because you will lead these people to inherit the land I swore to their ancestors to give them.**
>
> **Be strong and very courageous. Be careful to obey all the law my servant Moses gave you; do not turn from it to the right or to the left, that you may be successful wherever you go."** (Joshua 1:1-7)

God never intended for the people of Israel to only stay in the hills! He wanted them to take the whole land, and yet their fear and lack of faith prevented them from taking hold of this promise of God. We must believe that if they had boldly set foot in the plains with faith, that God would have overthrown the chariots and given them the whole land. Then they would have multiplied powerfully!

> *"Today, the 'geography' we are fighting for is not of only of limestone and granite, but the hearts of mankind!"*

What are the "hills" and what are the "plains" that we must conquer if we are to be successful in our conquest of world evangelism? Today, the "geography" we are fighting for is not only of limestone and granite, but the hearts of mankind! We are fighting for the hills of the spiritually poor, imprisoned, blind and oppressed, as well as the plains of the wealthy, the fortunate and the educated.

The most powerful and clear example of "fight from the hills" that I can think of comes from my dear brother, Raul Moreno, and his lovely wife, Lynda! Raul planted the São Paulo International Christian Church in Brazil in August 2011. In the first two years, about 18 disciples from what was left of the ICOC joined Raul to be part of the new movement. They formed the base of his ministry "in the hills."

Raul wasted no time and immediately set up camp at "Universidade de São Paulo" (USP). USP is the Harvard or Yale of Latin America. For five months, he, along with his mission team from Los Angeles, faithfully shared their faith every week day on this campus without a single baptism. Yet, Raul believed that wherever he placed his foot, God would give him. He very easily could have shifted his focus to the favelas or working class neighborhoods. However, he knew that if he could crack this top college, that the fountain of leadership would allow him to aggressively evangelize all of Brazil and Latin America.

The author's dear friend and partner in the Gospel - Raul Moreno. Raul is the seasoned Evangelist of Sao Paulo who has demonstrated an ability to flourish under adverse circumstances.

After those grueling five months, they finally baptized their first USP student, Danilo Bataglin, who was studying civil engineering! As of the writing of this chapter, Danilo has now graduated, married his beloved Carol, appointed Evangelist and he leads the West Region and the Campus Ministry of the São Paulo ICC with over 70 sold-out campus students! As of this moment, there are currently 35 disciples at USP! Among the veterans of the USP Ministry are Bia Hida, who leads the women of the South Region, and Vaitsa Haratsaris, who leads the East Region with another awesome campus student Tulio Amaral! Another USP graduate Caio Costa and Audrey Bravo are leading the recently planted Rio de Janeiro ICC! The USP Campus Ministry has created a flow of leaders who serve all over the church! To Raul and all the Brazilian disciples, "Bom trabalho!"

When I interviewed Raul for this chapter, he expressly asked me to emphasize that this strategy takes time and consistent hard work. However, if we stay the course and keep our feet planted, we will see incredible multiplication. With this kind of "plains" converts, one can build a ministry much larger than one would otherwise be able.

This is the fruit of "fight from the hills." It is about reaching and baptizing amazing "five-talent" people who can multiply our strength so that we can reach so many more! Once we have a few "five-talent" students at a table for a Bible study, we can easily engage the most influential people on the campus.

At the end of the day, how do we conquer the "plains" from the "hills?" (Joshua 1:3) *"I will give you every place where you set your foot, as I promised Moses."* Simply pour down from the hills and plant your feet!

Practically speaking, a very classic mistake made by leaders of small churches is to place their high potential intern on campus, but then they themselves wade into the fires and crises of the singles and marrieds ministry. Inevitably, a couple years in, they will find their ministry is stagnant or shrinking and they are discouraged. Rather, like Raul, if you are a small church leader, it is best to stay on the top campus yourself. Keep your inspiring Intern with you or send him to the lesser campus. Work in the marrieds and singles Bible Talks through mature House Church Leaders. Your House Church Leaders will then gain strength through experience and your campuses will flourish. Remember, your marrieds and singles may very well not mature because of your presence. Your campus will be crushed because of your absence. This "fight on the plains" takes discipline, sacrifice and conviction to maintain.

Off campus, how do we know if someone is a "five-talent" person? Because they are intimidating! That is the Spirit prompting us that we should reach out to them! If we do not do so, then we will fail to conquer the plains!

In closing, if we are alone like Jesus and walking by the Sea of Galilee, what are the hills we need to conquer? Are there disenfranchised ethnic groups that the majority looks down upon? Are we reaching out to the tradesmen and contractors? Are there parts of town where we would not want to walk around at night? Do we have a Bible Talk there? Jesus would! If we are not in the plains or even the hills - but flat on our faces - then like David at Adullam (1 Samuel 22:1-2), we need to get our cave in the hills, prey and begin evangelizing!

The clear majority of ministries are already in the hills! We do not need to fight for the hills if we have already conquered them! Too often ministries can get comfortable in the "hills" and are rarely able to grow beyond a certain point. How high can a building go if we are only using wood? Therefore, many churches become stagnant after they hit a certain membership number. Also, I believe God is not interested in exclusively multiplying in the hills. We should not expect God to bless a ministry that refuses to set foot on and conquer the plains. (Judges 2:2-5) If we are in the hills, it is time to pour down into the plains like our life depends on it!

We need to get a list of top campuses and start to plant them one by one. Get a list of the most prominent neighborhoods and plant Bible Talks in the well-to-do suburbs! In today's world of cheap transportation, the wealthiest people often live in commuter belts around the city. If we only have our Bible Talks in the inner city, we will not reach those well-to-do suburbs.

We can never forget that the goal of "fighting from the hills" is to take the hills and the plains - the whole Promised Land must be taken. This cannot be over-emphasized. The elite campuses, the wealthy neighborhoods, the sometimes aloof majority ethnic groups, must all be liberated for Christ. This conviction is not called "fight *in* the hills," it is "fight *from* the hills." Let us become an ethnically diverse church with Bible Talks on the mean streets, the main streets, the moneyed streets and every other street!

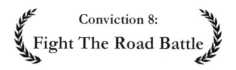

Conviction 8:
Fight The Road Battle

Have a plan to develop every corner of your area of responsibility!
See the farthest borders of the area God asks us to evangelize!
Travel and stretch your ministry geographically.

**Having an incredible time with the McKeans in Mexico
at the Latin American Missions Conference!**

*After this, Jesus traveled about from one town and
village to another, proclaiming the good news of the
Kingdom of God. The Twelve were with Him, and also
some women who had been cured of evil spirits and
diseases: Mary (called Magdalene) from whom seven
demons had come out; Joanna the wife of Chuza, the
manager of Herod's household; Susanna; and many*

others. These women were helping to support the Twelve out of their own means. (Luke 8:8-3)

This is an incredible passage about the ministry of Jesus. This traveling ministry of Jesus set the tone for all first-century Christianity. The early church was characterized and led by men and women who journeyed boldly from one place to another spreading the Gospel.

Carlos and Lucy Mejia the valiant leaders of the fast-growing Mexico City ICC!

When Paul wrote to the Corinthian Church, he said, *"...we, however, will not boast beyond proper limits, but will confine our boasting to the field God has assigned to us, a field that reaches even to you."* (2 Corinthians 10:13) Paul did not limit himself to the Antioch Church, which was his primary post. (Acts 11:25-26) Rather, he extended his reach to the whole field God had assigned him.

Matthew 10:5-6 says, *"These twelve Jesus sent out with the following instructions: 'Do not go among the Gentiles or enter any town of the Samaritans. Go rather to the lost sheep of Israel.'"* Again, Jesus was conscious of His field, and even when He sent out the disciples two by two, He always carefully delineated their field for them. Do each of our disciples know his or her field?

Paul writes in 2 Corinthians 11:26, *"I have been constantly on the move. I have been in danger from rivers, in danger from bandits, in danger from my fellow Jews, in danger from Gentiles; in danger in the city, in danger in the country, in danger at sea; and in danger from false believers."* He had the courage to preach the Word throughout his field even though it was dangerous and costly to do so.

In Luke 22:35-36, we find that Jesus emphasizes the same thing, *"Then Jesus asked them, 'When I sent you without purse, bag or sandals, did you lack anything?' 'Nothing,' they answered. He said to them, 'But now if you have a purse, take it, and also a bag; and if you don't have a sword, sell your cloak and buy one.'"* It is clear from this Scripture that the danger of the road is no excuse to fail to travel anywhere and everywhere, to bring the good news to every nook and cranny of our mission field. Ostensibly, disciples might have even had swords to ward off aggression from bandits!

One of the most exciting road battles that I have fought was during our planting of Paris, France, in August of 2013. In the three months that we were there, we saw many critical points of the city planted with Bible Talks. On the wall of our living room, we had a massive map of the city with thumbtacks showing all the current and future Bible Talks. After careful planning and seeking input, we built a project to have a Bible Talk at the four main "Gares" (train stations) that lead in and out of the city which were the nerve centers of the

Metro and bus system as well. We also included "Chatelet Les Halles," which is one of the main shopping areas in the center of the city, as well "Place D'Italy" which is a student ghetto.

We called our plan "The Jericho Project," as it circled Paris and made us available to everyone in the city. We issued color-coded project sheets to everyone in the church with maps and lists of the project. We mentioned it at almost every meeting and celebrated every time a new Bible Talk went out!

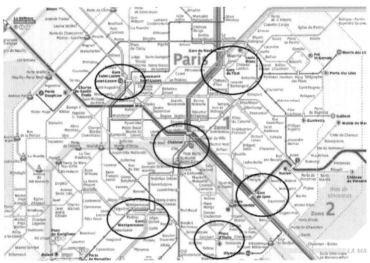

The Paris Underground map is circled showing the locations of the initial six Bible Talks of the Paris Church.

Before Lianne and I left due visa issues, there were only two more stations to get to before the Jericho Project was complete. We had a similar project for the campuses lead by our loyal armor bearers Anthony and Cassidy Olmos! We also envisioned a "region" of the church at Terrigny, which is a commuter city outside Paris. The Jericho Project was an exciting plan to saturate Paris, France, with Bible Talks. It resulted in thirteen additions in twelve weeks to the church in Paris - a city said to be one of the "hardest" mission fields in the world.

Anthony and Cassidy Olmos are a powerful couple with an exciting future serving the Lord in the ministry!

In Los Angeles in 2016, Lianne and I, along with our awesome Shepherding Couples, the Bordieris and Untalans, visited all 12 regions of the CAICC in Los Angeles, as well as the surrounding satellite churches of Southern California! It was an amazing time and we reached all the regions and churches in about three months! This allowed us to completely survey the churches, and therefore the project was named "The Walls of Jerusalem." It was critical to meet all the disciples in person and understand the opportunities and challenges of each ministry.

The author at the Taj Mahal in India.

Travel and movement are critical to Christian ministry. Right from the beginning of Acts, Jesus said, *"But you will receive power when the Holy Spirit comes on you; and you will be my witnesses in Jerusalem, and in all Judea and Samaria, and to the ends of the earth."* (Acts 1:8) Jesus called His disciples to evangelize the whole earth. This was the inspiring call known to every disciple in the first-century church - and this they did! Paul wrote in 62 A.D., *"This is the Gospel that you heard and that has been proclaimed to every creature under Heaven..."* (Colossian 1:23) Just as in the first century, we have the same mission today!

If we are the campus minister of our church, have we visited every campus in our city? As a ministry leader, do we know where all the neighborhoods are? Do we have a plan to reach them all? If we are a Bible Talk Leader in a neighborhood, have we walked along the border or been to the highest spot to survey and pray over our land?

Have we traveled to the surrounding towns to pull in the remnant and the "lost sheep of Israel?" It is interesting that so many former disciples "find themselves" living out in the towns and villages where rents and mortgages are coincidentally much cheaper. If that is where they are, that is where we need to go to get them! Altogether, this is what we call "fighting the road battle." We cannot allow our ministry to get "cornered," but we must expand our ministry as far as we can! Expansion is the "fun" of ministry!

"Fighting the road battle" means opening up new territory; however, it also gives us time - while we travel in cars, planes, buses and trains - to spend with our disciples, and to teach them in a way we might not have time for in the hustle and bustle of everyday life. This is a practical of Jesus' ministry to remember.

> "...if we want to see *local growth*, then it is *critical to preach and teach about global evangelism.*"

It is counterintuitive, but if we want to see local growth, then it is critical to preach and teach about global evangelism. Local groups become so inspired with global victories! Pounding, without vision, on the need for growth in a local group can create a negative and claustrophobic atmosphere. Building convictions on the need to grow so that we can save others is inspiring and encouraging! We must inspire our ministries and stretch our groups by calling them to reach other fields. The first-century church advanced locally and inspired their local groups by thinking globally. An excellent and practical tool to accomplish this is to have everyone read the monthly Good News Emails sent from Los Angeles by Kip.

Another way to train our disciples to "fight the road battle" is to "stretch" them and call them to attend regional and worldwide conferences and training sessions. These conferences are not a mission team, but they will get the disciples into the swing of picking up and traveling to other places for the purposes of the Gospel. They also give disciples the opportunity to fellowship disciples from other parts of the world and see churches from a global perspective. We should take every opportunity to get our ministry mobile and traveling. Of course, this does need to be balanced and tempered by the need to have fruitful local work.

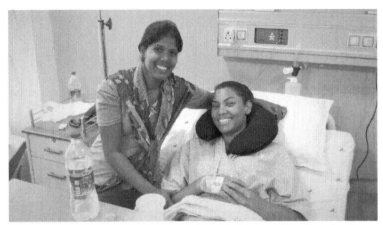

Lianne Kernan in the hospital in Chennai India after being diagnosed with Dengue Fever.

When we break into new territory, it is very wise to have a "reach-back group" of leaders who are experienced in the field we are entering. This is a council of people who know the language, culture, history and have experience of where we are going. They can advise us and help us to understand the obstacles we will face. We need to know our reach back group well, so that we have clear and easy communication. We should not try to build such a group after we are already in the field as it is often too late at that point.

We need to train ourselves, our family and our ministry to be expert travelers! Here are a few areas to consider:

1) Do we know important words in the local language? Do we have a translator and some good translation books?

2) Are our immunizations up to date? Consider getting your Yellow Fever, Meningitis, Typhoid Fever, Polio, Rabies, Flu, Td/Tdap, Shingles (if you are over 60 years old), Pneumococcal, Meningococcal, MMR, HPV, Chickenpox, Hepatitis A and B, and Hib vaccinations. Having served in the third world many times,

Lianne, the kids and I have had all the appropriate shots by age. Even with that, we have had serious medical emergencies on the mission field. In Chennai, Lianne was hospitalized with Dengue Fever and Tim Jr. with a serious tropical stomach virus. Both came close to death. Lianne and I will be forever grateful to the amazing prayer warriors - Raja and Debs Rajan - for their hospitality during these difficult days, especially how they took care of our son David. We never once worried about him because he was in their home. This is family.

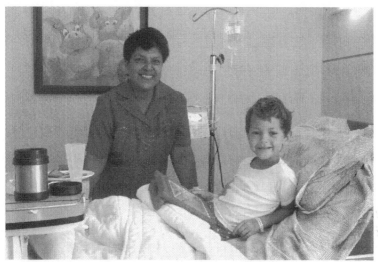

Tim Jr. hospitalized in India with a tropical stomach virus. He is accompanied by our wonderful sister "Auntie Grandma June."

3) Are we familiar with the medical world as it relates to our journey? We should know the medicines that we and our family will need. Before going on a trip, we need to consider things like asking our doctor to prescribe us some mild antibiotics just in case. There are various malaria pills and they all have different side effects - know them! We should not wait until we desperately need antidiarrheal, antihistamine, anti-motion sickness, pain or fever medicines (like

acetaminophen, aspirin, ibuprofen), laxatives (which we may need due to some of our other medicines), altitude sickness, antifungal and antibacterial medicines! We should have them all carefully stowed away in advance for when we will need them! We need to have our insect repellent, anti-bacterial wipes and gels, sunblock, aloe gel for sunburns (especially in my case) as well. We can laugh now, but if we do not go on a missionary journey with these items, we can be sure we will return with them! We need to know the medical dangers and have a small first aid kit with the medicine brands we know and trust. To evangelize the world, we cannot be well-intentioned newbies. That does not honor God or accomplish our mission.

**David Kernan enjoying a hot day
in Agra, Northern India.**

4) Are we equipped for the road? Does our passport need to be renewed? Do we have travel insurance? Do we have insurance on our flights? Do we have the right international travel package on our phone? Will it work when we arrive? Do we have a good satchel or backpack, walking shoes, hat, handy rain jacket/wind breaker, trusty sweater, laptop, power converter, power bar, battery packs, camera, voice recorder, money belt, hard water bottle, can opener, knife fork and spoon, weather appropriate and sturdy clothes, durable luggage,

sleeping bag, personal hygiene bag, street legal folding knife or multi-tool, (always put it in our luggage to get through airport security), flashlight, map of the area, and stationary kit. We should have a folder with all our vital documents, or notarized copies, so we can get visas or prove our identity if we must!

5) Do we know a little about the local botany, animal life, poisonous insects, snakes, etc.? We need to know a little about the geography, history and demographics. Every Bible Talk Leader should be the world expert on the square mile around their Bible Talk, and every missionary should be at least not clueless about where he or she is going!

6) Do we know in advance and/or have we trained those with us to know how we should react and respond to a mugging, corrupt officials, those begging for money or food, a medical emergency, etc.? We need to make sure everyone knows the plan regarding finances, schedule and where we will be sleeping. We need to ask ourselves these questions: Do we have a daily rendezvous point in case we are separated? Have we left our travel plans with trusted friends back home? Do we need to hire a local guide to help us? Best case is that we have a local disciple of course! In short, if we go on a missionary journey without planning in these areas, then we are planning to fail. We will spend more time simply trying to survive than actually preaching the Gospel!

7) While we are on our journey are we taking pictures, writing articles, uploading MP3 sermons, and letting all the local ministries back home and around the world know about the amazing things God is doing? These communications are motivating and inspirational for world evangelism!

As missionaries, we are liberators! Millions are depending on us to respond to God's call to go to the farthest corners of our assigned field and conquer the world for Christ. We cannot let a lack of vision, a lack of planning, or a lack of training prevent us from reaching a soul for Christ.

How we are dressed can affect how we are treated, even in war-torn countries!

Do we see our ministry as only the disciples in our group, or do we include the hundreds of thousands or millions of lost souls in our geographic area as well? They may not come out to church, but if they are in our field they are our ministry. What would happen if every disciple fought the road battle and extended the reach of the Gospel to the full limits they have been appointed? What would happen if we were *"constantly on the move"* (2 Corinthians 11:26) like Paul? Let us pull out our maps, research our fields, get a good pair of "sandals," and then conquer the roads that lead to so many lost souls!

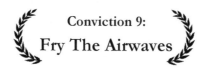

Conviction 9:
Fry The Airwaves

Take advantage of technology to advance an effective ministry!
Paul prayed sincerely for "open doors" to communicate the
Gospel. Modern information technology provides a
powerful open door for your ministry.

**In the darkest days of World War II, the British
Broadcasting Corporation (BBC) in London
sent a message of hope to Occupied Europe.**

Devote yourselves to prayer, being watchful and thankful. And pray for us, too, that God may open a door for our message, so that we may proclaim the mystery of Christ, for which I am in chains. Pray that I may proclaim it clearly, as I should. Be wise in the way you act toward outsiders; make the most of every opportunity. Let your conversation be always full of grace, seasoned with salt, so that you may know how to answer everyone. (Colossians 4:2-6)

This is such a lovable Scripture! Here, Paul is chained to a Roman soldier and under house arrest, and he prayed for an opportunity to proclaim the Gospel. Of course, the letter he wrote to the Colossian Church becomes Scripture, read by millions today. I would say his prayer was powerfully answered! Paul's desire to always look for an opportunity to proclaim the Gospel is so impressive.

We live in the "age of information." The average person today has more ways of communicating than a television station in the 1950's! Cell phones allow us to talk to almost anyone in the world, anytime. With email, we can send pictures, video, documents and sound files instantly. Twitter and Facebook permit us to publish our thoughts and quickly receive feedback. These developments in communication have created massive open doors for the Gospel.

Conversely, Satan has also seen the open door of communication technology. Through the Internet, he has spewed countless terabytes of pornography, hate, lies and abuse. Indeed, the Internet's "invisible continent" is as heathen as any other continent and desperately needs to be evangelized.

Of great concern is the assault on youth. The effect of the Internet on youth is overlooked by many as trivial or harmless, but by targeting youth, particularly on campus, with so much filth, massive damage can be done - and has been done - within one generation. However, the opposite can also become true. By impacting the youth of today, using whatever means of communication we have at our disposal, Satan's attack can be thwarted and overcome.

> *"By impacting the youth of today, using whatever means of communication we have at our disposal, Satan's attack can be thwarted and overcome."*

The fact is that only a small handful of disciples take full advantage of the open doors of communication made available by the Internet. This number needs to multiply rapidly, but it will take leadership to do so. So many disciples, upon baptism, restoration or placing membership, comment about how sermons, articles, videos and contact with disciples online made a decisive impact on their coming to the Lord. Over fifty percent (50%) of church leaders in the SoldOut Movement reported at the 2011 Global Leadership Conference that their first encounter with the SoldOut Movement was online, as many hail from our former fellowship. The facts are stunning, yet the response is lacking. The airwaves must be fried with the Gospel!

In the darkest and most sinister hours of World War II, when Hitler's shadow had enveloped Europe, Radio America and the BBC broadcasted a message of hope to those caught behind enemy lines. As freight trains hauled millions of men, women and children to death camps, and the Gestapo black-bagged all opposition, small groups of American and British agents filled the airwaves with hope from antennas in London and aboard ships in the Atlantic. For those going through the terrors of the occupation, listening to these channels on hidden radios gave life-saving hope to endure, to dream of freedom, and to fight on.

Today, just as in World War II, there are a few agents pouring out hope against the darkness: our CyberEvangelists in the SoldOut Movement, who shine like stars in the darkness. Ron Harding is the leader of our CyberMinistry, and to the forces of evil in the *"kingdom of the air"* (Ephesians 2:2), I am sure he is considered the deadliest "hacker" of cyberspace. Why? Ron does not hack into bank accounts, but rather into hearts, to give hope and encourage the faithful. By posting countless thousands of articles, pictures, videos and sermon mp3's, Ron has done more damage to the *"kingdom of the air"* than we may ever know.

**The original CyberEvangelists from left to right:
Jeremy Ciaramella, Rob Onekea
and Ron Harding.**

Joining Ron are Jeremy Ciaramella, who secures the sites from counter-hackers, and Rob Onekea, Elliot Svenkenson and Jake Studer, who make everything look great and attractive with their graphic art and videography skills. Not to mention, Lance Underhill, the king of social media with ICC Hot News! Joshua Ajayi, described as the new generation of CyberEvangelist, is highly qualified with a Computer Science Degree specializing in computer programming! I am the least of the CyberEvangelists and do not deserve to be called one; however, I am honored to be among them in this endeavor, doing what I can through photography, online videos, articles and sermons. So many people can be reached through the Internet, and yet there are so few focused on this opportunity.

The SoldOut Movement CyberEvangelists: (top from left to right) Jake Studer, Ron Harding, Jeremy Ciaramella, Rob Onekea, and (bottom from left to right) Joshua Ajayi, Lance Underhill and Elliot Svenkenson.

The Internet is about communication - if we have nothing to communicate, we are finished before we start. Therefore, the primary issue in web ministry is content. As a leader of a group of disciples, we are surrounded by amazing "content opportunities." As we preach the Word and see the results, we create incredible content. Sermons, worship, baptisms, restorations, placed memberships, friendships, families, weddings and celebrations are a constant part of our ministries. What we need now is people to write about, record, photograph and video all this content! One practical is to begin to videotape every sermon and then post them to YouTube!

After content, the next thing we need is a "quarterback," because principle or conviction without leadership is nothing. The best plan is often to choose a leader. Jesus' plan to evangelize the world is simply to put a disciple in every nation! The disciple will figure it out! We need to appoint a WebDeacon or WebDeaconess and "responsiblize" them. Consider having a weekly meeting, or a regular section in our leadership or Staff Meetings, to discuss and teach on the CyberMinistry. Do not delegate and disappear on your cyber staff. Be sure to review what the site and social media feeds look like and make sure you are happy with it.

In CyberMinistry, as Ron Harding often says, timing is paramount. *"A man finds joy in giving an apt rely - and how good is a timely word."* (Proverbs 15:23) For example, a sermon preached on Sunday morning should be posted by Sunday night at the latest. Experience tells us that nine out of ten visitors to a site will visit a page to look for a sermon and if it is not there they will not return. CyberMinistry is about windows of opportunity!

All this can be intimidating however even if we have no idea how to operate a website, then as the leader we must take responsibility and work though those who do have the skills. Most church leaders know that not every leader is a song leader, and yet they know how to work through a song leader to provide a great worship service. It is the same principle with the CyberMinistry. We cannot "delegate and disappear" thinking that a WebDeacon will "handle it." Would we do that in any other area of our ministries? We must delegate and follow through until the airwaves are fried with the message! If a sole WebDeacon cannot manage the entire ministry, then we need to form a team. If our team lacks training, we need to bring in a trainer and set up a seminar. If our seminars are not good enough, we need to go to other seminars. If that is not working, we need to bring in a trained WebDeacon. So many Christians are already incredible at social media, they just need to be directed to use their skills evangelistically! We need to assume responsibility and make it work!

One of the inspiring developments of 2016 was #ILoveMyChurchICC, which encouraged disciples to post amazing content all over the Internet and be able to easily search for other Christian content, like photos of baptisms, testimonies, celebrations, events, etc.! Another hashtag is #FIRE, which stands for "Faithful In Radical Evangelism!" Within a week of it being released, there were over a hundred powerful photos and videos of evangelism in action - all searchable through the same hashtag!

Another powerful technology revolution is the introduction of livestreaming in the major social media networks! Today, our favorite social media platform will allow us to livestream video around the world to an unlimited audience instantly from our phone! This is such a powerful resource! In fact, at our last Global Leadership Conference, our audience included individuals in 71 nations because of livestreaming!

There are so many other unconquered and underutilized platforms such as Instagram and LinkedIn.com - the chosen social media platform for millions of business people - which beckon for conquerors for Christ! The technology will continue to mature and become more powerful, the websites will change, but the main idea

- reaching the lost through whatever means possible - does not change!

> *As the rain and the snow*
> *come down from Heaven,*
> *and do not return to it*
> *without watering the Earth*
> *and making it bud and flourish,*
> *so that it yields seed for the sower and bread for the eater,*
> *so is my Word that goes out from my mouth:*
> *It will not return to me empty,*
> *but will accomplish what I desire*
> *and achieve the purpose for which I sent it.*
> (Isaiah 55:10-11)

As the leaders of our ministries, are we "frying the airwaves?" Do we regularly post our sermons on our site, our Twitter feed and our Facebook profiles? Do we keep them fresh with articles, videos and pictures? Can someone easily locate our services from the front page of our site? Can someone get in touch with us within one click from our site? Can someone catch the fire of faith and become a radicalized disciple from our online efforts? If the answer is no, then "fry the airwaves" is a strategy we must start to employ!

When we preach the Word through every open door, it will never come back empty! Preach the Word online and watch the fruit multiply! A dark world desperately needs our message!

Welcome to Part 4! Here is where we exceed expectations by building deeper convictions. We will look at building conversion power into our ministries at every level. We will learn how to stay surrounded by the people we want to convert and avoid becoming isolated. We will build deeper convictions on the power of preaching God's Word. We will learn more about worship and the critical role it must play in our lives and ministries. We will get a dream for serving and how it can unleash God's power! Let us go through these convictions one by one and take our ministries to the next level!

Conviction 10:
Build Conversion Power

Is every member of your ministry able to convert a lost soul? What do we need to do to turn every member, every group, every meeting and every resource into a powerful converting force?

Phillipe and Prisca Scheidecker baptizing their incredible daughter Rébecca in 2015!

Then the eleven disciples went to Galilee, to the mountain where Jesus had told them to go. When they saw Him, they worshiped Him; but some doubted. Then Jesus came to them and said, "All authority in Heaven and on earth has been given to me. Therefore go and make disciples of all nations, baptizing them in the name of the Father and of the Son and of the Holy Spirit, and teaching them to obey everything I have commanded you. And surely I am with you always, to the very end of the age." (Matthew 28:16-20)

This is an incredible Scripture detailing Christ's blueprint of the church. It is amazing that Christ saddles us with the huge responsibility of "making" disciples before He saves them! Per Jesus' plan, all disciples are to "make" disciples, who in turn would make more disciples and so on. It is a powerful plan based on exponential growth and widespread conversion power throughout the church to reach as many lost souls as possible.

Jesus Himself quickly developed the conversion power in His ministry and taught His disciples how to make disciples. In John 3:22 the Bible says, *"After this, Jesus and His disciples went out into the Judean countryside, where He spent some time with them, and baptized."* However, a little later in John 4:1-2 we read, *"The Pharisees heard that Jesus was gaining and baptizing more disciples than John, although in fact, it was not Jesus who baptized, but His disciples."* Jesus had trained His disciples to baptize and had moved on to supervising their training as baptizers. This was the focus of His ministry and He was willing to give His very life blood to multiply Himself in His 12 Apostles.

Is it optional to have a ministry that has strong conversion power? A little further on in John 6:29, when asked about the work of the Lord, *"...Jesus answered, 'The work of God is this: to believe in the one He has sent.'"* Again, in John 3:39-40, Jesus tells us God's will, *"And this is the will of Him who sent me, that I shall lose none of all that He has given me, but raise them up at the last day. For my Father's will is that everyone who looks to the Son and believes in Him shall have eternal life, and I will raise him up at the last day."* If it is God's will and God's work to bring people to Christ and keep them faithful, why should any ministry have a different goal?

In Matthew 28:19, Jesus says *"go"* make disciples. That means we cannot just wait for disciples to come to us. We need to take the message to them! Every disciple has this as their primary mission in life.

> *"If it is God's will and God's work to bring people to Christ and keep them faithful, why should any ministry have a different goal?"*

While we are unapologetically evangelistic and we believe that everyone we reach should give their lives to God, no one can or should be forced to make that personal decision. However, we can *"persuade"* (Acts 17:4), *"contend"* (Philippians 4:3), *"convince"* (Acts 28:23), *"reason with"* (Acts 18:4), and otherwise refute the lies that are holding someone captive to sin and away from God. As ministers we must work to change the minds of the lost and help them to see the truth. This is the heart of converting someone to Christ.

In 2 Corinthians 10:3-5 the Bible says, *"For though we live in the world, we do not wage war as the world does. The weapons we fight with are not the weapons of the world. On the contrary, they have divine power to demolish strongholds. We demolish arguments and every pretension that sets itself up against the knowledge of God, and we take captive every thought to make it obedient to Christ."* The Bible has the divine power to overcome any argument that is holding someone captive to sin. This is such a powerful truth that needs to be taken hold of and applied by every disciple! The truth is that conversion power is a synonym for "liberation power."

On a wall in the Museum of Natural Science in Chicago, there is a checkerboard with 64 squares. In the lower left-hand corner is a grain of wheat. The display includes this question, "If you doubled the amount of wheat as you move from square to square, how much would you have when you reached the 64th square? A carload? A trainload? No. You would have enough wheat to cover the country of India six feet deep." A grain of wheat makes a grain of wheat. A disciple must be able to make a disciple. That is the impact of conversion power. We just need more people to believe in it!

> *Since, then, we know what it is to fear the Lord, we try to persuade others... For Christ's love compels us, because we are convinced that one died for all, and therefore all died. And He died for all, that those who live should no longer live for themselves but for Him who died for them and was raised again...*
>
> *All this is from God, who reconciled us to Himself through Christ and gave us the ministry of reconciliation: that God was reconciling the world to Himself in Christ, not counting people's sins against them. And He has committed to us the message of reconciliation. We are therefore Christ's ambassadors, as though God were making His appeal through us.* (2 Corinthians 5:11,14-15, 18-20)

The very fear of the Lord motivates us to persuade others. Why? We do not want people to fall into God's judgment. Also, we are compelled, literally the word means "to have no choice," to be ambassadors of Christ because of His awe-inspiring love for us!

It is not easy to put this heart into every disciple in our ministry, but we must! We must train every disciple to persuade others and be a personal ambassador of Christ! It will take great preaching, focused discipling times and a terrific example to get every member to be a daily evangelistic force of nature!

In my personal ministry, this has been one of my greatest failings. Recently in a discipleship time with Kip, while attending the incredible Latin American Missions Conference in Mexico City, he lovingly confronted me about my personal lack of evangelistic example. I had forgotten the Scriptures above and needed to be called back to the standard. I was heartbroken to see how right he was. I was very grateful that he loved me enough to talk to me about this need for repentance. At that moment, I set my heart to have a guest at church every week and had a guest at church eleven weeks in a row. One week my guest cancelled on me at the last minute so I went out and shared my faith in the fellowship break! The young lady who I reached out to turned out to have studied the Bible with disciples before and drifted but is now committed to studying again! God works when we truly devote ourselves to Him. God is awesome I am not.

I went on to challenge every member of the World Sector to follow my example of evangelistic repentance. It is amazing how a confession and repentance can sometimes have more impact than a command! I am very cut by my failure to live up to this quote that I love from General George S. Patton, *"Always do everything you ask of those you command."* It stings me even now that I failed so badly in this regard.

As we train our ministry in this teaching, there will no doubt be stumbles and falls. Some will teach incorrectly and will make mistakes. We are building a heart, a conviction and a lifestyle of evangelism and converting. We must be unrelenting and bold. We must roll up our sleeves and set our hearts to this task to build an abundantly fruitful ministry. (John 15:8) Thi will not happen overnight, but with focus and time, we will absolutely achieve it!

> *Now, Lord, consider their threats and enable your servants to speak your Word with great boldness. Stretch out your hand to heal and perform signs and wonders through the name of your holy servant Jesus.*
>
> *After they prayed, the place where they were meeting was shaken. And they were all filled with the Holy Spirit and spoke the Word of God boldly.* (Acts 4:29-31)

We need always to keep in mind that evangelism, to be successful, requires *"great boldness!"* We can say the right things, but without transferring our heart, we cannot have the desired outcome. Keep the fight in your evangelism! Supervised group sharing times are indispensable to ignite individual evangelism. Make sharing times fun! Effective fruitfulness requires enthusiasm, passion, boldness and zeal, but they must all be tempered and contained within a respectful, loving and gentle delivery. (1 Peter 3:15)

Every ministry will have a few people who can convert. However, deliberately generating an ever-increasing conversion power means that every element of the ministry must be scrutinized, assessed and strengthened.

Are we setting an example in our personal evangelism? The more people with whom we share, the more people who have a chance to respond to the Gospel. We need to take an honest assessment of how much evangelism we do in our ministry. Reaching out to the lost world is so important to us as disciples that we do it daily. Even when under serious physical persecution and attack the Apostles example is challenging, ***"The Apostles left the Sanhedrin, rejoicing because they had been counted worthy of suffering disgrace for the Name. Day after day, in the temple courts and from house to house, they never stopped teaching and proclaiming the good news that Jesus is the Messiah."*** (Acts 5:41-42) We need to consider what we need to do to make this Scripture come to life in our ministries. Never change the standards to where you "are at," but rather change where you "are at" to meet the standards! Are we setting an example ourselves by bringing guests to our Bible Talk and Sunday services consistently?

Joe and Kerry Willis are incredible examples of personal evangelism! They consistently spend long hours on campus reaching out to students.

Have we taken our disciples along with us evangelizing so that they can become confident reaching out to strangers? Are our disciples evangelistically effective on campus? We need to ask ourselves: Is it a training issue? A faith issue? Whatever the issue may be, we need to stay on it until we have attained fruitful and daily evangelism.

Have we trained our disciples to overcome objections that people may raise? We need to teach and train on the false doctrines that are out there. Perhaps even develop a library and a rebuttal book of good Biblical responses to the lies that Satan is using to hold people in slavery. (One of my next books, *Assaulting The Gates Of Hell* does just that!) Just as a martial artist collects "moves," we collect rebuttals and ways of convincing people to come to God. As Peter said, *"But in your hearts revere Christ as Lord. Always be prepared to give an answer to everyone who asks you to give the reason for the hope that you have. But do this with gentleness and respect, keeping a clear conscience, so that those who speak maliciously against your good behavior in Christ may be ashamed of their slander."* (1 Peter 3:15-16)

Are we a Jew to the Jew and a Greek to the Greek? Being able to overcome objections is critical, but our disciples must also be trained to deal with different types of people. What will get a more rational person interested in the Bible? What about a more emotional person? Should an introverted person be spoken to in the same way as someone who is more outgoing? Will people from different walks of life be reached out to in the same "cookie cutter" way? We must *"become all things to all men."* We need to use anything we can to help us build conversion power.

Is every disciple in our ministry trained and confident in their First Principles? Hebrews 5:11-12 teaches, *"We have much to say about this, but it is hard to make it clear to you because you no longer try to understand. In fact, though by this time you ought to be teachers, you need someone to teach you the [First Principles] of God's Word all over again. You need milk, not solid food!"*

Often, a ministry that has low "conversion power" is a ministry that lacks a rock-solid knowledge of the First Principles[8] at every level. Churches and ministries that baptize and retain are groups in which every member is trained to teach the First Principles. Every member must be taught the Scriptures well and become teachers who follow the *"pattern of teaching"* (2 Timothy 1:13) that was taught to them.

In Los Angeles in 2016, we initiated "Project Blacksmith." This name is from 1 Samuel 13:19, which says, ***"Not a blacksmith could be found in the whole land of Israel, because the Philistines had said, 'Otherwise the Hebrews will make swords or spears!'"*** During this project, we converted our alternating Men's and Women's Midweeks into First Principles Classes taught by the lead couples! The women taught the women and the men taught the men for several months until every region completed the entire course! This had an immediate knock-on effect, as now every member was trained to study with and convert a lost soul!

Is teaching aimed at the hearts of visitors at all Sunday services, Bible Talks and meetings of the church? We cannot be afraid to plead with people to study the Bible! We cannot be afraid to warn people of God's wrath! (Acts 2:40) We need to work this into every sermon! In our preaching, we should constantly remind the disciples of what it was like before their baptisms so they can remember how dark the darkness was! What we focus on is what we will get. If we focus on preaching to the hearts of the lost, it is the hearts of the lost that we will win.

As our ministry grows and multiplies numerically because of all the conversions, then we will have the bonus of "move-ins" to our ministry who will come because they want to participate in the miracles that are happening! Conversely, if we are not converting, we

---

[8] Kip McKean "First Principles", Discipleship Media (Jan 2012) Available at www.usd21.org

will get "move-outs" who want to be used by God somewhere else! As Jesus said, ***"Whoever has will be given more, whoever has nothing even that will be taken away."*** (Mark 4:25)

Fruit that will last! Levi Pettigrew (Cal State Long Beach Theta Chi Fraternity President) of the South Region!

As disciples, we believe that anyone can change, and there is no one with whom we will not study the Bible. We are not looking for people who are already doing great; rather, through the Scriptures, we aim to raise people up so that they will "do great!"

Conversions must be conversions that will last! Even before someone is baptized, we need to consider who is going to disciple them after baptism. This person needs to be worked into the studies. It is so important to make sure that he or she has an excellent relationship with the discipler-to-be in his or her life and that there is an ease of communication and teaching between them.

Matthew 28:20 is often overlooked; but Jesus taught that we must not only be baptizing, but also *"...teaching them to obey everything I have commanded..."* We follow up with and strengthen new disciples so that we are adding disciples who will learn to be great "evangelizers" and in turn make other disciples. In particular, we have five "Follow Up Studies" - written by Kip and in our First Principles Booklets - that are geared to do exactly that! However, a mistake so many make is to stop after these "Follow Up Studies" and fail continue to have dynamic discipling times. A lack of follow-up can devastate the conversion power of a ministry.

From John 4:1-2 we learn, *"The Pharisees heard that Jesus was gaining and baptizing more disciples than John, although, in fact, it was not Jesus who baptized, but His disciples."* Jesus baptized those who were already disciples, not those who simply pledge to be disciples. How do we know if someone is ready to be baptized? We know when he or she has begun to live his or her life as a disciple! (Matthew 28:19) Have they begun to give financially? Have they begun to evangelize? Are they truly open? Are they building great friendships? Only baptize disciples, not those who merely wish to be!

Remember, conversions are essential to our mission. However, as has been mentioned previously, if we are converting but not raising up new leaders who lead new Bible Talks and ministries, then we will not multiply. Conversions are additions; new Bible Talks are multiplication. This is a truth that can take many painful experiences to understand fully! Every ministry must have a seed of another ministry inside it! As the famous Scottish author Robert Louis Stevenson once said, "Don't judge each day by the harvest you reap but by the seeds that you plant." Does every Bible Talk Leader have a right-hand person who is getting ready to begin their own Bible Talk? Is every Evangelist training a young intern? Does every Deacon have an apprentice? If these seeds are not planted, then there will be no multiplication power and, in fact, the ministry will begin to diminish.

"Truly, truly, I say to you, unless a grain of wheat falls into the earth and dies, it remains alone; but if it dies, it bears much fruit." (John 12:24) What is it going to take to make conversion power happen? A lot of dying to self. We can never forget this point. Conversions and numerical growth in the ministry come from tears more than any other factor. If disciples are not willing to die to themselves by making others more important than themselves, then abundant conversions will not happen. Are we ready to die for baptisms?

> *"Growth... comes from tears more than any other factor."*

We need to stay focused on our conversion power until we have achieved the ability of being effective in this area, not only among the leaders, but at every level of the church! Conversion power is not one thing - it is prayer, sacrifice, teaching, pleading, warning and the forceful moving of the Holy Spirit. We all want ministries that are abundantly fruitful. So, we need to think about our evangelism from how much to how effectively our we are sharing our faith. We must have feet on the street that are able to overcome objections. We need to think about our competence in teaching the First Principles. We need amazing "Counting Of The Cost Studies" that help people to make decisions they understand and will stick with for life. We need strong follow-up that makes converts into strong converters in turn. Let us start building conversion power into our ministry today!

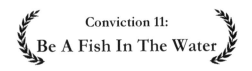

Conviction 11:
Be A Fish In The Water

Get closer to the people we want to influence! People surrounded Jesus all the time, but modern life can isolate and "quarantine" us. Turn that around!

Kyle and Joan Bartholomew lead the evangelization of the Pacific Rim and live in Manila, Philippines.

A few days later, when Jesus again entered Capernaum, the people heard that He had come home. They gathered in such large numbers that there was no room left, not even outside the door, and He preached the Word to them. Some men came, bringing to Him a paralyzed man, carried by four of them. Since they could not get him to Jesus because of the crowd, they made an opening in the roof above Jesus by digging through it and then lowered the mat the man was lying

on. When Jesus saw their faith, He said to the paralyzed man, "Son, your sins are forgiven." (Mark 2:2-5)

In this passage in Mark, we see the fascinating closeness Jesus had with the people. Jesus seems to have constantly been surrounded by large crowds. In several Scriptures, he actually seems to have taken steps to get away from the crowds, including a boat escape! (Matthew 13:13) Jesus was no wallflower! He was the most charismatic person to ever walk the face of the earth! He was comfortable dining with tax collectors, (Matthew 9:10) attending weddings (John 2:2), and hosting picnics with 5,000 of his closest friends! (Mark 6:41) Even though He focused on "the few" - teaching the 12 - crowds gathered to listen! (Matthew 5:1)

The word charisma comes from the Greek *"carisma,"* which means "divine gift" or "divinely given ability." Without a doubt, the ability to attract so many people is truly a God-given talent! It is a skill for which every minister should strive.

> *"Of course, for any band of preachers and teachers, isolation is death!"*

Of course, for any band of preachers and teachers, isolation is death! Being surrounded by the people was and is a matter of survival for Jesus' ministry. It is an amazing thing how well Jesus managed and orchestrated events so that throngs of people constantly surrounded His disciples. To someone who is not looking for it, the masterful work of Jesus in this regard might be easy to miss.

In Acts 2:46-47, we see that the church carried on Jesus' way of life:

Every day they continued to meet together in the temple courts. They broke bread in their homes and ate together with glad and sincere hearts, praising God and enjoying the favor of all the people. And the Lord added to their number daily those who were being saved.

Again, in Acts 5 we read:

Crowds gathered also from the towns around Jerusalem, bringing their sick and those tormented by impure spirits, and all of them were healed... Day after day, in the temple courts and from house to house, they never stopped teaching and proclaiming the good news that Jesus is the Messiah. (Acts 5:16, 42)

We see that they were surrounded by people and winning their favor through their way of life. Daily, the disciples were getting into the social centers and even the living spaces of the people of Jerusalem! This is the ultimate example of how disciples should be operating.

In fact, the first-century disciples not only lived close to the people they wanted to influence, but they also lived within those communities. In a sense, the first-century church exploded along pre-existing social channels. The main three were the synagogue, the house church network and the campus!

Paul and all of the Apostles evangelized from within the synagogue. A little-known fact is that it was two hundred years after the resurrection of Christ that the Christians were fully ejected from the

Judaism as a whole.[9] This was a very fruitful channel of relationships for the early disciples.

The author preaching in English with Hindi translation from Johnson Gona!

Another network that the disciples worked through was that of "House Churches." (Colossians 4:15; 1 Corinthians 16:19) Greco-Roman architecture favored large villas with a community kitchen and even a community worship room. When disciples would move into one of these buildings, they would quickly evangelize everyone and essentially connect it to their network of "House Churches" that disciples already lived in.[10] Today, people live much more isolated lives due to the changes in modern architecture.

---

[9] James D. G. Dunn, *Jews and Christians: The Parting of the Ways* by Durham-Tubingen Research Symposium on Earliest Christianity and Judaism (2nd : 1989 : University of Durham),
[10] Wayne A. Meeks, *The First Urban Christians: The Social World of the Apostle Paul* (New Haven and London: Yale University Press, 1983), pp. 30-31.

Another first-century channel, or network, that is still explosive today is the campus ministry. When Paul was expelled from evangelizing the local synagogue in Acts 19:9, he then headed to the campus! *"Some of them became obstinate; they refused to believe and publicly maligned the Way. So Paul left them. He took the disciples with him and had discussions daily in the lecture hall of Tyrannus."* To this day, disciples are spreading the Gospel from campus to campus! The first-century disciples entered pre-existing social communities and converted them wholesale or in part. Campus students: Are we living in the dorms and hosting Bible Talks there?

We see this principle again in Matthew 9: 9-11:

> *As Jesus went on from there, He saw a man named Matthew sitting at the tax collector's booth. "Follow me," He told him, and Matthew got up and followed Him.*
>
> *While Jesus was having dinner at Matthew's house, many tax collectors and sinners came and ate with Him and His disciples. When the Pharisees saw this, they asked His disciples, "Why does your teacher eat with tax collectors and sinners?"*

Here we see how Jesus masterfully turned a "cold contact" - a meeting with someone without a regular reason for doing so - into a "warm contact" - a meeting of friends with friends. This is a huge strategy that is not fully employed today. Jesus was a master of charisma and a true "fish in the water" of humanity.

The one to coin the term "fish in the water" was Mao Zedong of China. In his book on how he fought the far superior Japanese forces in China in World War II, Chairman Mao Zedong once wrote:

Many people think it impossible for revolutionaries to exist for long behind enemy lines. Such a belief reveals a lack of comprehension of the relationship that should exist between the people and the revolutionaries. The former may be likened to water, the latter to the fish who inhabit it. How may it be said that these two cannot exist together? The people are the sea in which the revolutionary swims. The revolutionary must move amongst the people as a fish swims in the sea. It is only undisciplined workers who make the people their enemies and who, like the fish out of its native element, cannot live.

Chairman Mao's revolutionary forces infiltrated thousands of villages in China behind the lines of the occupying Japanese. Through a persistent campaign of winning villages to his cause, he was able to mount "hit-and-run" attacks and ambushes against the Japanese, like ghosts attacking from the darkness. His guerrillas - hiding and living among the people - exhausted and eventually defeated the Japanese Imperial Forces. They were successful because, to the Japanese, they were indistinguishable from the civilian population. They denied the Japanese any decisive victories, and they prolonged the conflict until the Japanese retreated due to financial exhaustion. Essential to their strategy was that they behaved in a way that won the villagers' hearts and minds to their cause. They had surrounded themselves in a sea of people and moved about freely among them like a fish, even though they were in purpose distinct from the people.

As Christians, we are fighting a spiritual "revolutionary war," and the principle is clear that isolation is death for any group that wishes to advance its cause among the people. If we want to grow numerically, then we must fight against being "quarantined" from the hearts and minds that we wish to impact. Without purposeful and copious contact with dozens and dozens of people each day, a local minister will be choked out (Matthew 13:22) and eventually fade away.

Practically speaking, if we are sharing with someone who is part of the PTA or a basketball team on campus, what is to stop us from going to their meeting before we ask them to come to ours? Cold contact must be turned into warm contact as soon as possible. We need to reach past the person we are evangelizing and meet their friends as well, just like Jesus did. Far too often Satan quarantines disciples from the community by preventing cold contact from becoming warm contact. Disciples need to get actively involved in "community life." We need to use sports or hobbies - any other preexisting network of people - to turn our cold contacts into warm contacts!

As disciples, we have all had to change our lives and rid ourselves of self-destructive and dangerous ways of living. Some have thrown out the "baby with the bathwater" and no longer pursue their interests and hobbies! The consequence is their life is not as enjoyable and they fail to connect with the hundreds and thousands of people around them! Satan has prevented them from having a powerful impact! Paul went straight to the synagogue to preach because that was his community. It was a sinful one, but he brought many Jews to believe and many God-fearing Gentiles as well. The same can happen today!

Why not set up a Christian professionals' luncheon or regularly attend a business professionals' luncheon? Why not create a Christian craftsmen and tradesmen breakfast, or even attend a non-Christian one? As Jesus said in Matthew 10:11, *"Whatever town or village you enter, search there for some worthy person and stay at their house until you leave."* What is the "town" and "home" you need to enter?

For the most part, the disciples did not build churches from scratch, but turned pre-existing social communities (synagogues, private homes, villages, lecture halls, etc.) into the powerful "churches" of the first century! There are pre-existing communities out there, and we can and must imitate the first-century disciples and "infiltrate" them instead of only limiting ourselves to bringing people into the church one by one.

Even in the church itself, ministers can become isolated. Never allow a "clergy/laity divide" to form. ***"Whoever claims to live in Him must live as Jesus did."*** (1 John 2:6) All disciples are called to be like Jesus. While some disciples are paid and others are not, our mission is the same. When the fellowship divides into the clergy and the laity, it is the death knell of true discipleship. This is the denominational church model where the "pastor" does all the work.

Even between churches in the same movement, disciples can become isolated. This is the work of the Devil who wants to isolate and then destroy these churches. We must ensure that disciples do not only have great friendships in their local church, but that they feel close with members of our surrounding churches. Facebook and other social media can create the perfect venue for this. As well, let me stress again the need to attend Missions Conferences around the world!

We need to draw in members by seeking and soliciting advice from our tradesmen and our professionals. Every disciple is a minister and we need to stay close to our non-paid workers so we can draw not only from them but their non-Christian colleagues as well. For lack of a better word, leaders must be expert "love bombers!" When we run into someone outside the church, when someone comes to our fellowship, we need to be able to impact them with our genuine love, interest, curiosity and care. Sometimes all a ministry needs to get going is a little good old-fashioned (and sincere) love-bombing!

When our persecutors accuse us of love-bombing, I say, "Don't knock it until you've tried it!"

It takes time to learn to surround ourselves with people and become experts at turning cold contacts into warm contacts. It takes planning and conscious effort to live amongst the people we want to impact. If we are campus ministers, do we live right next to the campus so we can have people over to our homes and be present on campus for long hours during the day?

Remember, it is impossible to fit discipleship into our lives; instead, we need to fit our lives into our discipleship. (Luke 9:23-24) What other activities might we need to curtail to spend more time *"among the crowds," "in the temple courts,"* or *"going house to house?"* When the Israelites asked for time to worship their God, Pharaoh said in Exodus 5:8-9, *"They are lazy; that is why they are crying out, 'Let us go and sacrifice to our God.' Make the work harder for the people so that they keep working and pay no attention to lies."* Satan has the same program today. He wants us working so hard we have no time or energy for God.

Do we live frugally enough that we can make ends meet without working so many hours that we have no time to be around people? The "larger" we live, the larger the amount of work we must put in to afford that lifestyle. As disciples who want to be around as many people as possible and preaching God's Word as much as possible, we must ask ourselves: "How cheap can we live?" As campus interns, if the church was paying us half a monthly salary and we were making another half from a part-time job, could we spend the rest of our time on campus getting to know people?

Even if we are full-time ministers, we can get caught up with all kinds of things that can take away from our greatest priorities:

In those days when the number of disciples was increasing, the Hellenistic Jews among them complained against the Hebraic Jews because their widows were being overlooked in the daily distribution of food. So the Twelve gathered all the disciples together and said, "It would not be right for us to neglect the ministry of the Word of God in order to wait on tables. Brothers and sisters, choose seven men from among you who are known to be full of the Spirit and wisdom. We will turn this responsibility over to them and will give our attention to prayer and the ministry of the Word."

This proposal pleased the whole group. They chose Stephen, a man full of faith and of the Holy Spirit; also Philip, Procorus, Nicanor, Timon, Parmenas, and Nicolas from Antioch, a convert to Judaism. They presented these men to the Apostles, who prayed and laid their hands on them.

So the Word of God spread. The number of disciples in Jerusalem increased rapidly, and a large number of priests became obedient to the faith. (Acts 6:1-7)

Here we see that the number of disciples was *"increasing."* However, after the Apostles reprioritized their lives to focus on their personal worship and the preaching of the Word amongst the people, the number of disciples *"increased rapidly."* No ministry can grow *"rapidly"* if the leadership does not have the right priorities and the time to get in amongst the people to preach God's Word!

We must never let growth intimidate us. *"So neither the one who plants nor the one who waters is anything, but only God, who*

makes things grow." (1 Corinthians 3:7) Just like the Apostles, we must plant and water with all our hearts. Just like a baby, every ministry by nature will grow because this is what God wants them to do. If a baby is not growing then there is a serious problem that needs to be addressed. Remove the problem, add the nutrition, and God will continue to grow the baby and our ministries are the same thing. You cannot grow a ministry unless you have the time to plant and water it.

All this aside, proximity and persistence are of no value if we do not have the loving charisma of Jesus. Jesus' righteousness - His fulfillment of every duty of every relationship - made Him attractive to the people around Him. We must determine to imitate Jesus until the crowds feel this way about us!

Can we live among the people? Can we live closer to the people? Can we live cheaper so we have more time to work for the Lord? Can we focus more on making disciples daily? Jesus had a dream of disciples "swimming" among the people of all nations. Let us make it a reality in our generation!

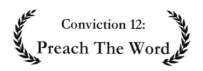

Conviction 12:
Preach The Word

The Word of God is always the solution to every problem. What do I need to learn about preaching the Word?

Cory Blackwell, one of the most compelling preachers of our generation, preaching a lesson in Long Beach, California!

In the presence of God and of Christ Jesus, who will judge the living and the dead, and in view of His appearing and His Kingdom, I give you this charge:

Preach the Word; be prepared in season and out of season; correct, rebuke and encourage - with great patience and careful instruction. (2 Timothy 4:1-2)

What a powerful Scripture and charge! In God's presence, and in eager expectation of the coming day of the Lord, we are given a critical responsibility. That sacred duty is to share God's life-giving Word with all of mankind! We are called to be always ready to preach with impact and precision! What an amazing role with which we have been entrusted!

We can sympathize with the powerful young prophet Jeremiah who said,

> *"A disciple who has powerful, early morning times in the Scriptures and prayer will radically share God's Word that is within them!"*

Whenever I speak, I cry out proclaiming violence and destruction. So the Word of the Lord has brought me insult and reproach all day long. But if I say, "I will not mention His Word or speak anymore in his name," His Word is in my heart like a fire, a fire shut up in my bones. I am weary of holding it in; indeed, I cannot. (Jeremiah 20:8-9)

This man was a prophet on fire for God! He was so full of the Word of the Lord that he was not able to contain it regardless of people's reactions! A disciple who has powerful, early morning times in the Scriptures and prayer will radically share God's Word that is within them! Only with consistent times in the Word of God can we be ready to preach with fire!

In Jeremiah 1:17-19, God tells the young prophet:

"Get yourself ready! Stand up and say to them whatever I command you. Do not be terrified by them, or I will terrify you before them. Today I have made you a fortified city, an iron pillar and a bronze wall to stand against the whole land - against the kings of Judah, its officials, its priests and the people of the land. They will fight against you but will not overcome you, for I am with you and will rescue you," declares the Lord.

Preaching the Word is the incredible duty and honor of all leaders in God's Kingdom. God will give us the strength to effectively communicate His Word! God can make us like a *"fortified city,"* unassailable by the enemy hoards; an *"iron pillar"* to carry the bone crushing pressure that can come in ministry; a *"bronze wall"* to stand against any siege machine or arguments that this dark and depraved world may throw at us!

In Romans 6:17 we read, *"But thanks be to God that, though you used to be slaves to sin, you have come to obey from your heart the pattern of teaching that has now claimed your allegiance."* In 2 Corinthians 2:9 Paul writes, *"Another reason I wrote you was to see if you would stand the test, and be obedient in everything."* The Word of God is reduced to mere "information" on the lips of a preacher who lacks the courage to call for obedience as God commands! In Romans 1:5 the Bible says, *"Through Him we received grace and Apostleship to call all the Gentiles to the obedience that comes from faith for His name's sake."* The Scriptures must always be preached with an expectation of faith and obedience! A true preacher applies God's Word and is as demanding and commanding as Jesus was.

Devote yourselves to prayer, being watchful and thankful. And pray for us, too, that God may open a door for our message, so that we may proclaim the mystery of Christ, for which I am in chains. Pray that I may proclaim it clearly, as I should. Be wise in the way you act toward outsiders; make the most of every opportunity. Let your conversation be always full of grace, seasoned with salt, so that you may know how to answer everyone. (Colossians 4: 2-6)

Even though Paul was chained and under guard, he was still praying and asking others to pray for God to open a door so that he could preach the Word. Nothing could prevent Paul from preaching and looking for openings for the Gospel. As ministers our life is looking for "ways and means" to get the Gospel through to people's hearts in a clear and compelling way. This takes great prayer and according to this passage, it takes group prayer to succeed!

Now, Lord, consider their threats and enable your servants to speak your Word with great boldness. Stretch out your hand to heal and perform signs and wonders through the name of your holy servant Jesus. After they prayed, the place where they were meeting was shaken. And they were all filled with the Holy Spirit and spoke the word of God boldly. (Acts 4:29-31)

The Word of God is not only preached with an expectation of obedience and through every door with clairity, but it must also be preached with *"great boldness!"* Preaching without passion and zeal is not preaching at all, it is at best, "explaining." Disciples were never called to merely inform people of God's Word, but to change the world with it. We must keep the fight in our preaching, understanding the spiritual battle that we are in. When speaking to a large crowd I often imagine myself in a debate with Satan fighting to win the hearts and minds of the audience from his grasp.

**The McKeans, Williamsons and Kernans enjoying
a time of fellowship at Buckingham Palace
in London, England.**

Not only must we preach with boldness but also with love for *"...a gentle tongue can break a bone."* (Proverbs 25:15) Boldness without love is harsh and destructive. Boldness with love can move even the hardest heart. *"Therefore encourage one another and build one another up, just as you are doing."* (1 Thessalonians 5:11) If we talk to our audience like they are failures that is what they will be. If we talk to them the way we would talk to our favorite sports team or other people we really respect then they will rise to our expectations! When we preach switch the "do you" phrases to "we are!" Which is better? "Do you share your faith? Or "Jesus died for us and this lost world! That is why we are sharing our faith! It is who we are!" "Speaking up" to the audience and giving them respect and encouragement is so important!

"Rescue those being led away to death; hold back those staggering toward slaughter." (Proverbs 24:11) Do not be deceived, the world we see today is the result of generations without a movement that is committed to preach God's Word **"with power, with the Holy Spirit and deep conviction."** (1 Thessalonians 1:5) Indeed, the world is the way the world is because the church is the way the church is. We must rescue as many as possible from this **"corrupt generation."** (Acts 2:40) Preachers must emerge with the heart to urgently stop those who are stumbling toward more and more pain!

Do not be mistaken, every human right we have, every concept that gives dignity, equality, tolerance and justice, comes from the Scriptures and not from man. Without the inherent truth that man is made in the image of God (Genesis 1:27), we are relegated to being mere animals. The foundation of laws in the Western world is based on the Biblical understanding of mankind as a special creation of God. That is why in the United States there are constitutionally entrenched terms like "In God we trust" and "One nation under God."

For example, it was the Bible that first said men and women are equal.

> *So in Christ Jesus you are all children of God through faith, for all of you who were baptized into Christ have clothed yourselves with Christ. There is neither Jew nor Gentile, neither slave nor free, nor is there male and female, for you are all one in Christ Jesus.* (Galatians 3:26-28)

I challenge anyone to find anything about equality between common men and women in any human writings that existed before the Scriptures. (*Hammurabi's Code* that seems to say something about equality of women only relates to very wealthy and well-born women.) Yet sadly, many modern feminists are anti-Christian. They have stepped away from God's perfect will and have tried to make men and women not only equal, but the same. The consequence is dysfunction, divorce and unattractive and unappealing relationships amongst men and women that have caused the generations that follow to struggle with homosexuality. The following Scripture is so true of our society!

Jesus is persecuted to this day!
(courtesy of reddit.com)

The wrath of God is being revealed from Heaven against all the godlessness and wickedness of people, who suppress the truth by their wickedness, since what may be known about God is plain to them, because God has made it plain to them. For since the creation of the world God's invisible qualities - His eternal power and divine nature - have been clearly seen, being understood from what has been made, so that people are without excuse.

For although they knew God, they neither glorified Him as God nor gave thanks to Him, but their thinking became futile and their foolish hearts were darkened. Although they claimed to be wise, they became fools and exchanged the glory of the immortal God for images made to look like a mortal human being and birds and animals and reptiles.

Therefore God gave them over in the sinful desires of their hearts to sexual impurity for the degrading of their bodies with one another. They exchanged the truth about God for a lie, and worshiped and served created things rather than the Creator - who is forever praised. Amen.

Because of this, God gave them over to shameful lusts. Even their women exchanged natural sexual relations for unnatural ones. In the same way the men also abandoned natural relations with women and were inflamed with lust for one another. Men committed shameful acts with other men, and received in themselves the due penalty for their error. (Romans 1:18-27)

As the Biblical foundation of our society crumbles, we will continue to slide ever more into the gutter - the pagan society from which we came. The only thing we can do to prevent this is to send disciples into every community in the world and have them preach God's Word convincingly!

As Jude wrote, *"But, dear friends, remember what the Apostles of our Lord Jesus Christ foretold. They said to you, 'In the last times there will be scoffers who will follow their own ungodly desires.' These are the people who divide you, who follow mere natural instincts and do not have the Spirit."* (Jude 17-19) These *"last times"* are these times! I truly believe that if and when "modern liberalism," atheism and commercialism finishes eradicating the Christian influence of our laws and culture, it will land mankind in even deeper darkness and pain. In that world only those who can afford them will have justice, equality, dignity and safety.

"Gay Pride" marches are now common place around the world.

We must fight this dark future with everything we have. Preaching the Word of God is confronting and demolishing the lies that enslave the people in our families, our schools and our communities. (2 Corinthians 10:3-5) The Word of God has divine power to demolish arguments and pretensions that set themselves up against God's *"good, pleasing and perfect will"* for our lives. (Romans 12:2) That makes preaching the Word of God one of the most incredible things we can do!

Learning to convey God's Word powerfully is an important responsibility as well. ***"Do your best to present yourself to God as one approved, a worker who does not need to be ashamed and who correctly handles the Word of truth."*** (2 Timothy 2:15) We must seek training to proclaim God's Word effectively, be it through public speaking or writing. Natural talent will only take us so far, but truly effective, long-term impact comes only with training and hard work. Write and rewrite your sermons and lessons until you master them.

Not only must our preaching be persuasive and accurate, but it must also be compelling. God's Word must always be presented as it is - exciting, challenging and inspiring! Preaching the truth in a boring and un-captivating way plays straight into Satan's scheme. When we preach, we need to be larger than life and deliver our message like the ambassadors we are!

We need to engage whatever audience we have in an appropriate manner. Campus Bible Talks should be different from those geared towards a group of married couples. There is nothing worse than a small group Bible Talk being preached like the main speech of a large congregational service!

In Japanese, there is a term "umami" which means "the point of deliciousness." It is the moment when we bite into a piece of perfectly prepared sushi, for example, and are compelled to say "ahhhhh!" It is the "wow" factor. The point of deliciousness is reached when food is perfectly prepared and served.

I learned this word from a 2011 documentary by David Gelb called, *Jiro Dreams of Sushi*. This movie is about a sushi chef named Jiro Ono - a living legend - who has a very small restaurant in Tokyo which seats only ten people. His sushi is so good that each one of his ten coveted seats is constantly in demand. In fact, reservations must be made three months in advance, and one must reserve all ten seats! The meal is three hundred dollars per person and lasts but twenty minutes!

The documentary covers the training of Jiro's chefs at his tiny restaurant: the painstaking selection of the fish, the hours of preparation, and the final and beautiful presentation that invariably leads to happy restaurant patrons.

I asked myself as I was watching the beautiful cinematography, what if every preacher prepared for every Bible Talk, every debate and every lesson like this? What if every point in every lesson hit the "umami" point of deliciousness? How many more people would be saved?

Not only is preaching exciting and awesome for guests and visitors, but preaching from the Scriptures equips and trains everyone in the church for everything we should do in life and ministry. *"All Scripture is God-breathed and is useful for teaching, rebuking, correcting and training in righteousness, so that the servant of God may be thoroughly equipped for every good work."* (2 Timothy 3:16-17) In ineffective ministries, the Bible is taught but not applied, and the direction of the church is explained but not preached. We must take our direction straight out of the Word of God and preach it from the mountaintop at every opportunity!

When we preach the direction of the Scriptures with an expectation of obedience God's Word will go out and come back fruitful. I love this quote from John T. Walsh, a restoration movement preacher, "We want more faith and less machinery, more work and less talk, more faith and less planning. The Lord has given us a plan, and bids us to go work in His vineyard..."[11] Good preaching is about getting people to action, not filling the room with mere talk.

It is so inspiring when we preach the conquest of the Promised Land, the rebuilding of Jerusalem, or the defeat of Goliath and apply it directly to our local situation. When disciples can place themselves directly in the Scriptures because of our preaching, they advance like men and women on fire! Help people find themselves in the Scriptures. Are we in Mark 1 calling everyone off their boats? Are we in John 3:22 teaching everyone how to baptize? Are we in John 4 overseeing a powerful ministry? Are we in Matthew 28 sending them out? We need to always know where our ministry is in the Scriptures!

The challenge for church leaders is to train every disciple to preach the Word of God. It is incredible how learning to preach changes people! In fact, it changes the whole ministry when we have trained many preachers! One practical way to do this is to use midweeks and prepare disciples to preach short ten-minute lessons! Everyone will come ready to preach! This gets more "bang for our buck" out of our midweeks and is an exciting opportunity for every disciple!

Before calling someone up to preach at midweek a one point sermon, be sure to explain the importance of having a great title, the powerful reading of Scripture, proper explanation of what they just read, great illustrations and practical applications. We need to set our people up for victory. If we do, we will be blown away by their incredible sermons!

Another practical comes from the first volume of the epic series, *The Search For The Ancient Order*. In these volumes we are given a pearl of wisdom from our forefathers. After two debates with

---

[11] *The Search for the Ancient Order. Vol 2. page 60*

denominational preachers, it was written: "Indeed, these two debates convinced Campbell that a week's debating is worth a year's preaching."[12] This is an incredible element of preaching that far too many overlook. Debating is preaching! Jesus debated; Paul debated; the Apostles debated; and if we are to have the same impact that they did, then we too must debate.

It is understood that a disciple of Jesus needs to know his or her Scriptures very well. Weak Bible knowledge is a massive impediment to great preaching. We should read our Bibles from cover to cover every year. As well, we need to voraciously read more and more reputable commentaries and books about the Bible. We must build a culture of talking about the Bible, distilling its principles, and discovering the threads of teaching that are woven through it. This is the life of a preacher.

In 1 Corinthians 9:16 Paul writes, ***"Yet when I preach the Gospel, I cannot boast, for I am compelled to preach. Woe to me if I do not preach the Gospel!"*** We live in a world that has become deceived and entangled in Satan's schemes. That is why preaching God's Word is so important! Neglect of this duty is tantamount to collaborating with Satan and can only be attributed to cowardice or lukewarmness at the very least. Let us never be counted amongst the tepid souls!

Preach the Word through every door that God opens! Preach against the lies that are holding people down! Preach the Bible as our playbook, and preach the direction from it! Teach everyone to preach! Preach with an expectation of obedience! This is the call of a disciple and the greatest need of a dark and hurting world! Let us go forward preaching God's Word with faith and power!

---

[12] *The Search for the Ancient Order. Vol 1. page 66*

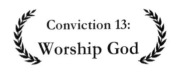

Conviction 13:
Worship God

All good things in ministry start with a profound worship of God.
Bring true, deep worship and praise into your ministry.

Omar Theranciel leading the Paris disciples in prayer.

Psalm 96:1-10 states:

> *Sing to the Lord, praise His name;*
> *proclaim His salvation day after day.*
> *Declare His glory among the nations,*
> *His marvelous deeds among all peoples.*

For great is the Lord and most worthy of praise;
He is to be feared above all gods.
For all the gods of the nations are idols,
but the Lord made the Heavens.
Splendor and majesty are before Him;
strength and glory are in His sanctuary.
Ascribe to the Lord, all you families of nations,
ascribe to the Lord glory and strength.
Ascribe to the Lord the glory due His name;
bring an offering and come into His courts.
Worship the Lord in the splendor of His holiness;
tremble before Him, all the earth.

This Royal Psalm teaches us the true attitude we need to have as followers and worshipers of God. True worship is to bow down and tremble before God as we consider how to please Him, bring offerings to Him, remember His power and might, praise His amazing deeds for us, and declare them to the nations! Worshiping God sums up so much of what we do as disciples! One lens to look at the ministry through is the power of moving the ministry through moving God. As John Causey often says, "Move God to move the ministry!" Consider the whole ministry though this lens!

What is worship? The word worship in this Scripture is a translation of the Hebrew word "shachah," which means "to physically bow down or prostrate oneself." However, worship has always been more than just getting down on your knees. In Romans 12:1-2 Paul writes:

> *Therefore, I urge you, brothers and sisters, in view of God's mercy, to offer your bodies as a living sacrifice, holy and pleasing to God - this is your true and proper worship. Do not conform to the pattern of this world, but be transformed by the renewing of your mind.*

191

Then you will be able to test and approve what God's will is - His good, pleasing and perfect will.

So *"true and proper"* worship is not only prostrating ourselves physically before God and worshiping Him verbally, but as Paul writes here, worship is found in the sacrificing of our lives and the renewing and transforming of our minds. We become *"living sacrifices"* who please God with every aspect of our lives. It is only then that we can truly know God's *"good, pleasing and perfect will."* I must believe that if anyone knows God's good, pleasing and perfect will, they would want to worship Him even more!

We should never think that there is some strategy that can help the most dedicated disciples to succeed without true worship. Although, as leaders we are called to have Biblical insight, deep convictions and great plans, we can never expect victory without true and proper respect for and worship of God.

How seriously does God take worship? Let us look at this passage:

> *The Lord said to Moses, "When you return to Egypt, see that you perform before Pharaoh all the wonders I have given you the power to do. But I will harden his heart so that he will not let the people go. Then say to Pharaoh, 'This is what the Lord says: Israel is my firstborn son, and I told you, 'Let my son go, so he may worship me.' But you refused to let Him go; so I will kill your firstborn son.'"* (Exodus 4: 21-23)

Here we see that Pharaoh's unwillingness to let God's people worship Him resulted in very serious consequences. This should give us pause as leaders and cause us to reflect on how our leadership brings people to worship God. Do we bring people to fall prostrate before the Lord and worship Him with true worship?

> *"Everyone either worships God or idolizes something else."*

The truth about human nature is that everyone wants to worship something. People who "struggle" to worship the Lord or claim that they worship nothing deceive themselves. Everyone either worships God or idolizes something else. Not only does everyone worship, but everyone wants to bring others to worship the same thing that they do. Idolatry is a communicable disease.

> *If your very own brother, or your son or daughter, or the wife you love, or your closest friend secretly entices you, saying, "Let us go and worship other gods" (gods that neither you nor your ancestors have known, gods of the peoples around you, whether near or far, from one end of the land to the other), do not yield to them or listen to them. Show them no pity. Do not spare them or shield them. You must certainly put them to death. Your hand must be the first in putting them to death, and then the hands of all the people. Stone them to death, because they tried to turn you away from the Lord your God, who brought you out of Egypt, out of the land of slavery. Then all Israel will hear and be afraid, and no one among you will do such an evil thing again.* (Deuteronomy 13:6-11)

The people of God must take idolatry seriously. It is the antithesis of worship. Consider this Scripture,

> *Son of man, these men have set up idols in their hearts and put wicked stumbling blocks before their faces. Should I let them inquire of me at all? Therefore speak*

to them and tell them, "This is what the Sovereign Lord says: 'When any of the Israelites set up idols in their hearts and put a wicked stumbling block before their faces and then go to a prophet, I the Lord will answer them myself in keeping with their great idolatry. I will do this to recapture the hearts of the people of Israel, who have all deserted me for their idols.'" (Ezekiel 14:1-6)

Today, we live in the New Testament period where idolaters are not killed but exclude themselves from membership in the Kingdom of God. The Bible instructs us to *"put to death, therefore, whatever belongs to your earthly nature: sexual immorality, impurity, lust, evil desires and greed, which is idolatry. Because of these, the wrath of God is coming."* (Colossians 3:5-6) Most of today's idolatry is not that of worshiping small statues, although that does exist in some cultures. Idolatry is the worshiping of sin in one's heart. (Ezekiel 14)

Although in the Western world we do not often see the worship of statues, there is a horrific level of consumerism and materialism, which is also idolatry. Even good things like education and jobs or cell phones, which allow us to communicate as never before, can become idols if we put them before God! We now have a generation who are enslaved to these things and who calculate their worth by their resume, possessions, popularity and credit report more than what it cost to purchase them from sin. Idolatry is truly a cruel slave master.

Conversely, as in George Orwell's famous book *1984*, Satan not only controls the oppression, in this case consumer idolatry, but also the apparent "resistance" to it. Today, the resistance movement to consumerism is the idolatry of nature. Nature does reflect the Divine; it was created by the Divine and we can learn so much about

God from it. As the Scripture says: *"For since the creation of the world God's invisible qualities - His eternal power and divine nature - have been clearly seen, being understood from what has been made, so that people are without excuse."* (Romans 1:20) Adam was made to work in the garden with nature. However, today Satan has perverted man's relationship with nature into one of abuse and idolatry. Do not have any illusions, nature is made by God and is awesome, but also dangerous. Nature can burn us, sting us, freeze us, infect us, dehydrate us, eat us, leech us, poison us, plant eggs in us and grow plants with our corpses. God made nature but nature is not God. Nature does not love us. We should not look to the sun or the moon or flowers or a forest for love or peace, but rather look to God.

Nature must be respected, admired, learned from, stewarded, protected and harnessed responsibly to make it fruitful and useful for God's people. People talk about saving the planet. The planet does not care if it has oxygen or not. In no way does it need saving. On the other hand, we need to save the planet's environment so that we can breathe! The godless world that we live in has either idolized nature or abused it. Only if the people of earth understand nature from a Biblical perspective can we save our habitat.

The true church of God is not only a church with the right doctrine, but a church where people have smashed the idols in their hearts; where they have offered themselves as living sacrifices; where there is true worship of God that is accompanied by singing, praising and exalting of God! *"Sing joyfully to the Lord, you righteous; it is fitting for the upright to praise Him. Praise the Lord with the harp; make music to Him on the ten-stringed lyre. Sing to Him a new song; play skillfully, and shout for joy."* (Psalm 33:1-3) Our true worship must always walk hand in hand with joyful praise! Worship services need to be incredible, life-changing events! Sunday service needs to be a worship experience our members and guests never forget!

As we meditate on true worship and humbling ourselves before God, let us consider the amazing leadership of Abraham Lincoln and his address to the American people:

By the President of the United States of America.

A Proclamation.

Whereas, the Senate of the United States, devoutly recognizing the Supreme Authority and just Government of Almighty God, in all the affairs of men and of nations, has, by a resolution, requested the President to designate and set apart a day for National prayer and humiliation.

 And whereas it is the duty of nations as well as of men, to own their dependence upon the overruling power of God, to confess their sins and transgressions, in humble sorrow, yet with assured hope that genuine repentance will lead to mercy and pardon; and to recognize the sublime truth, announced in the Holy Scriptures and proven by all history, that those nations only are blessed whose God is the Lord. And, insomuch as we know that, by His divine law, nations like individuals are subjected to punishments and chastisements in this world, may we not justly fear that the awful calamity of civil war, which now desolates the land, may be but a punishment, inflicted upon us, for our

presumptuous sins, to the needful end of our national reformation as a whole People? We have been the recipients of the choicest bounties of Heaven. We have been preserved, these many years, in peace and prosperity. We have grown in numbers, wealth and power, as no other nation has ever grown. But we have forgotten God. We have forgotten the gracious hand which preserved us in peace, and multiplied and enriched and strengthened us; and we have vainly imagined, in the deceitfulness of our hearts, that all these blessings were produced by some superior wisdom and virtue of our own. Intoxicated with unbroken success, we have become too self-sufficient to feel the necessity of redeeming and preserving grace, too proud to pray to the God that made us!

It behooves us then, to humble ourselves before the offended Power, to confess our national sins, and to pray for clemency and forgiveness.

Now, therefore, in compliance with the request, and fully concurring in the views of the Senate, I do, by this my proclamation, designate and set apart Thursday, the 30th day of April, 1863, as a day of national humiliation, fasting and prayer. And I do hereby request all the People to abstain, on that day, from their ordinary secular pursuits, and to unite, at their several places of public worship and their respective homes, in keeping the day holy to the Lord, and devoted to the humble discharge of the religious duties proper to that solemn occasion.

All this being done, in sincerity and truth, let us then rest humbly in the hope authorized by the Divine teachings, that the united cry of the Nation will be heard on high, and answered with blessings, no less than the pardon of our national sins, and the restoration of our now divided and suffering Country, to its former happy condition of unity and peace.

In witness whereof, I have hereunto set my hand and caused the seal of the United States to be affixed.

Done at the City of Washington, this 30th day of March, in the year of our Lord one thousand eight hundred and sixty-three, and of the Independence of the United States the eighty seventh.

By the President: Abraham Lincoln

What a bold letter and what reverence for God! If a political figure can call a nation to revere God, how much more so for Christian leaders in the Kingdom of God? We must usher true worship into our ministries like the rushing waters of a powerful river! Our leadership must start and finish with God and every powerful thing that worship means.

To achieve success in worship, we need to bring worship into the life of every individual disciple and our ministry as a whole. Everyone in our ministry needs to come to truly understand the nature and importance of worship! It does not mean adding more meetings to our calendar, but it might mean "digging down" deeper in the worship that we already have. Can our singing be more powerful? Can the prayers we already pray at the beginning and end of our meetings be more solemn or more joyful? Can we organize fasting for important situations, goals and ministry decisions? What about an all-night prayer and worship time? Can our personal quiet times become more worshipful?

Do we know how serious God is about worship, or are we relying on our strengths or insights? Do we worship God alone or are there other idols in our hearts that need to be smashed? Are we bringing our people to worship God physically and in terms of changing their characters and hearts for Him?

> *A time is coming and has now come when the true worshipers will worship the Father in the Spirit and in truth, for they are the kind of worshipers the Father seeks.* (John 4:23)

Worship is not only in prayer and singing, but also in deep personal change and sacrifice. Worship can change our ministry like nothing else if we can bring everyone to understand its power and apply it in their everyday life!

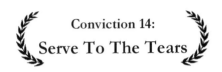

Conviction 14:
Serve To The Tears

Release the full potential of your ministry through your service!
What if everyone gave all they could and took only what they
needed? What if everyone was constantly learning new
ways to serve? What if our neighbors
shed tears from our service?

**Nick and Denise Bordieri work tirelessly for the poor and
underprivileged as MERCY *WORLDWIDE* Leaders.**

*Offer hospitality to one another without grumbling.
Each of you should use whatever gift you have received
to serve others, as faithful stewards of God's grace in
its various forms. If anyone speaks, they should do so
as one who speaks the very Words of God. If anyone*

serves, they should do so with the strength God provides, so that in all things God may be praised through Jesus Christ. To Him be the glory and the power for ever and ever. Amen. (1 Peter 4:7-11)

Here, Peter shows us a masterpiece of unlimited power: A Kingdom in which everyone serves. Imagine if everyone in the world unlocked their ability to serve others by giving all they could and taking only what they needed. The world would change so dramatically overnight that all history before it would pale in comparison! In a nutshell, this is the revolutionary dream of Christians. We do not believe in military, political, economic or even cultural solutions to the world's problems. As disciples, we share a revolutionary dream that if everyone would live like Jesus and serve like Jesus, the world would be *"on earth as it is in Heaven."* (Matthew 6:10) We believe this is the only solution to the world's problems.

Some people just have a gift for loving and serving! Travis and Cecy Frazier are such people and Congregational Shepherds of the CAICC!

You know that the rulers of the Gentiles lord it over them, and their high officials exercise authority over them. Not so with you. Instead, whoever wants to become great among you must be your servant, and whoever wants to be first must be your slave - just as the Son of Man did not come to be served, but to serve, and to give His life as a ransom for many. (Matthew 20:25-28)

Jesus wants a Kingdom of servants. Some have misunderstood this Scripture as Jesus saying we should not want to be great. Rather, He is showing us the road to greatness, which is service to others. What would the church be like if everyone was trained to be a powerful servant? Service to others is something that defines us as disciples. Albert Einstein once said, "The high destiny of the individual is to serve... The value of a man should be seen in what he gives and not in what he is able to receive." Excellent servants are thoughtful, skilled, productive and loving. They strive to learn how to serve in new ways and be excellent at everything they do. Excellent servants are excellent human beings and excellent disciples.

Sometimes we find ourselves in a state in which we think we have done everything we can to advance the ministry, and yet it is just not moving the way we would like. It is at times like this that we need to ask ourselves if the dream of service is alive and well in our ministries.

Other times as ministry leaders, we can say, "I've given everything I have to serve, and still things are not moving!" Perhaps we understand the importance of service and sacrifice, yet we have not called everyone else in our ministry to serve with the same heart and passion as we do. Someone who shares Jesus' dream of service will expect and teach that others serve in the same way. How much of the "service potential" in our ministry has been unlocked?

> *"It is very hard to have forceful advancement without effective servants."*

It is very hard to have forceful advancement without effective servants. General Dwight D. Eisenhower once said, "You will not find it difficult to prove that battles, campaigns and even wars have been won or lost primarily because of logistics." That is a powerful quote. Without the servants supplying, moving and maintaining the army, it will fail. A U.S. Marine Corps Officer, General Robert H. Barrow, once wrote, "Amateurs talk about tactics, but professionals study logistics." Indeed, many a great adventure has failed by outrunning the ability of the adventurers to supply and fund the demands of the effort.

It is a tremendous honor to be numbered among the hard-working administrators of the City of Angeles International Christian Church!

Administrators do so much of the serving when it comes to preparing our church financial, administrative, logistical, and legal plans. As church leaders, we may not have an MBA, but we do need to be able to oversee and be responsible for this important area of service. Can we answer the following questions?

1. What is incorporation and is our church incorporated?
2. Does the country, state or province we are serving in require special church permits or charity permits?
3. Does the church have the correct bank accounts for its type of organization? Have we gone down to the bank to meet our banker and seek advice?
4. Do we know how the taxes are paid every month? Remember, every time we pull money from the account for salaries, the tax man wants his share! Do we know how that works?
5. Do all our staff have their visas up to date if they are foreign workers? When do they need to be renewed? How are they renewed? Visas are a highly important area for international missionaries.
6. Does our staff have life insurance, pension plans and medical coverage? Take time with our admin(s) and meet the reps from these companies to at least become familiar with how these things work and their importance.
7. Have we combed through our financial plan and budget for the year? We cannot work a church budget on a napkin or in our head no matter how smart we are! We need to update our budget weekly! We need to know our monthly income and expenses!
8. Do we have our calendar laid out for the year ahead so that upcoming events do not surprise our members or budget planners?

These are a few questions that every church leader needs to be able to navigate. We may or may not have the skills of an admin, but if we are to oversee admins as church leaders, we must not be completely "un-savvy" in these areas. These are some of the questions that a leader needs to ask himself as he serves his ministry. Some of these things might seem very daunting; however, God will give us the strength to *"...discharge all the duties of your ministry."* (2 Timothy 4:5)

Service is also a very powerful evangelism tool! Jesus served the people around Him in extraordinary ways. Healing, feeding and teaching was the daily routine for Jesus. As a result, the people became (at least for a while) very protective of Him! So much so that John records, *"Yet, for fear of the Jews no one spoke openly of Him."* (John 7:13 ESV) This principle of service - earning the loyalty and protection of the people - is alive and well today, but sadly, not in "Christendom" at large. It is hard for Westerners to hear about and accept that terrorist groups like Hamas, Hezbollah and the Taliban put this principle into practice better than we do as Christians. The reason these murderous groups are so hard to eradicate is that they are protected by the population who love them and feel indebted to them because of their service. Wikipedia says of Hezbollah's social services:

> (Hezbollah) ...has social development programs, hospitals, news services, and educational facilities... Social services have a central role in the party's programs. Most experts believe that Hezbollah's social and health programs are worth hundreds of millions of dollars annually. The American Think Tank Council on Foreign Relations also said that Hezbollah "is a major provider of social services, operating schools, hospitals and agricultural services for thousands of Lebanese Shiites."

Though they use this loyalty for evil purposes, Hezbollah is "serving to the tears" of the Lebanese who surround them. Can our neighbors say the same of our Bible Talk? If we feel like we are facing a brick wall in terms of reaching out to our local community, why not try serving the community we are evangelizing? While people might stop us from sharing the Gospel with them, rarely will they stop us from serving them. Can we serve our way into a person's heart, into a community, or even into a mission field where overt missionary activities are illegal or are not having the desired outcome? As Francis of Assisi once said, "Preach the Gospel at all times. When necessary, use words." Sometimes people need to be preached to by our service before they will listen to our words.

Sadly, the terrorist group Hezbollah enjoys wide support among the Lebanese people because of their excellent service programs.

Practically, can our Bible Talks do more benevolent work? What about a dedicated MERCY*WORLDWIDE* Bible Talk that could serve at a soup kitchen, for example, and then use a table for a traditional Bible discussion? These are minimalist ideas, but the sky is the limit!

> *There is no need for me to write to you about this service to the Lord's people. For I know your eagerness to help, and I have been boasting about it to the Macedonians, telling them that since last year you in Achaia were ready to give; and your enthusiasm has stirred most of them to action. But I am sending the*

brothers in order that our boasting about you in this matter should not prove hollow, but that you may be ready, as I said you would be. For if any Macedonians come with me and find you unprepared, we - not to say anything about you - would be ashamed of having been so confident. So I thought it necessary to urge the brothers to visit you in advance and finish the arrangements for the generous gift you had promised. Then it will be ready as a generous gift, not as one grudgingly given.

Remember this: Whoever sows sparingly will also reap sparingly, and whoever sows generously will also reap generously. Each of you should give what you have decided in your heart to give, not reluctantly or under compulsion, for God loves a cheerful giver. (2 Corinthians 9:1-7)

Another powerful way to serve is to raise funds! This is a *"service for the Lord's people"* and requires great skill to motivate, inspire, encourage and find creative ways to raise funds for missions and special needs in the church. Paul said he would be *"ashamed"* if the people were not ready to give, but inspires them to be generous! Some find this duty to be distasteful, and in their minds, it can make them struggle! However, I love Joe Willis, the Sydney Church Leader, who stated, "Being asked to give does not make you struggle. It shows you are struggling!" Giving financially is an important way to "serve to the tears!"

As leaders, we provide an important service in raising funds for the Lord's people. The hard work for the leader begins many months before the funds are due. We must always cover our goal with pledges long before the deadline! As the Bible says in 1 Timothy 6:17-19:

Command those who are rich in this present world not to be arrogant nor to put their hope in wealth, which is so uncertain, but to put their hope in God, who richly provides us with everything for our enjoyment. Command them to do good, to be rich in good deeds, and to be generous and willing to share. In this way they will lay up treasure for themselves as a firm foundation for the coming age, so that they may take hold of the life that is truly life.

First, be sure we personally are obeying this Scripture before calling anyone else to it. Then, with the moral authority that comes from example, we must *"command those who are rich"* to be generous! Be very careful not to over delegate this task to others. As a rule of thumb, the directly responsible appointed Evangelist and/or Women's Ministry Leader should be having these conversations.

Once the membership has agreed to an amount to be given, then comes the hard work of organizing tagging, bake sales, garage sales, etc., so that they do not have to pull the money from their own pocket, but instead from outside fund raising! That being said, often the goal can be too large to cover with fund raising activities alone and everyone will have to pull from their own wallet. Noble plans like mission team sendoffs, the support of poorer churches or the hiring of staff can be very expensive. Look at King David's attitude to sacrifice, *"But the king replied to Araunah, 'No, I insist on paying you for it. I will not sacrifice to the Lord my God burnt offerings that cost me nothing.'"* (2 Samuel 24:24) God rewards this sacrifice! *"And do not forget to do good and to share with others, for with such sacrifices God is pleased."* (Hebrews 13:16) Organizing and managing fundraising well prevents crushing pressure on the church at the last minute.

In general, how does one train others to be excellent at service? While there are many things to consider, it is certainly true that these six "Ps" are among them! 1) A servant must be: **Prayerful** and connected to God (Philippians 4:4); 2) A servant must do things **Properly** the first time and not have to go back and undo shoddy work. (1 Corinthians 14:40) Proper also means ethical. As Andrew Smellie has said, "Intelligence is no substitute for integrity." 3) A servant is **Precise,** using accuracy more than power or force. (Ecclesiastes 10:10; 1 Thessalonians 5:12-14) 4) A servant is not fast or slow, but **Prompt,** knowing that speed and doing things at a "good clip" is important to success! (Isaiah 40:29-31) 5) A servant is **Private**. (Proverbs 11:13) People must have utmost confidence in our discretion. Evangelists are people who preach and proclaim, but if someone confesses to us or we are privy to sensitive information we take it to our grave without fail. 6) A servant is **Productive** (Psalm 126:4-6) and never just busy! These are qualities and skills of a servant and a leader. Someone who has mastered them will never be unemployed!

To paraphrase and "baptize into Christ" the bellicose quote of General George Patton, "One leadership skill that will never change is the importance of using whatever means are at hand to have the greatest impact in the minimum amount of time." This is the mindset of a true servant.

One incredible area in which service bears great fruit is in Sunday School Programs for children. Serving the "Kingdom Kids" is one of the acts of service most appreciated by parents and children. It is an area that immediately makes many members feel loved. The "kids" almost always become disciples, and the parents are incredibly grateful to the teachers who instilled a love of God in them from a very early age. It is by the hard work and dedication of servants that these programs survive.

When people have the heart of servants, they bring glory to God. However, when people are self-focused and entitled, they prevent the advancement of ministry. As Sun Tzu once wrote, "The general who advances without coveting fame and retreats without fearing disgrace, whose only thought is to protect his country and do good service for his sovereign, he is the jewel of the kingdom."

What could we do in the Kingdom of God with 5,000 skilled servants? What would happen in the world if everyone served like Christ? Let us unlock the power of service in our ministry!

★★★★★

He who overcomes will inherit all this, and I will be his God and he will be my son. (Revelations 21:7)

We are in the final stretch! Six more Bible convictions! A wise disciple once said, "the only thing that changes in life is the quality of your problems." We are going to learn to relish adversity, further the Gospel, deepen our understanding of family, sound the call to decision, and remain solid in the grace! Let us round out our learning and finish strong!

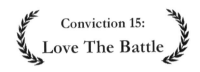

Conviction 15:
Love The Battle

Use defeats and setbacks as God intended: to train you all the way to victory. There are no problems in the ministry, only costs, lessons and opportunities.

Interns join the author in learning about the spiritual battle through physical battle!

In your struggle against sin, you have not yet resisted to the point of shedding your blood. And you have forgotten that word of encouragement that addresses you as sons:

"My son, do not make light of the Lord's discipline, and do not lose heart when He rebukes you, because the Lord disciplines those He loves, and He punishes everyone He accepts as a son."

Endure hardship as discipline; God is treating you as sons. For what son is not disciplined by his father? If you are not disciplined (and everyone undergoes discipline), then you are illegitimate children and not true sons. Moreover, we have all had human fathers who disciplined us and we respected them for it. How much more should we submit to the Father of our spirits and live! Our fathers disciplined us for a little while as they thought best; but God disciplines us for our good, that we may share in His holiness. No discipline seems pleasant at the time, but painful. Later on, however, it produces a harvest of righteousness and peace for those who have been trained by it. (Hebrews 12:4-11)

What an amazing Scripture this is! ***"Endure hardship as discipline"*** is a line that jumps out because it is so contrary to how we normally think of hardship. Trouble is training; God either directly brings it on us or allows it. In both cases God uses it to make us better! Today, we live in a society that regards pleasure and sentimentality as the highest state of "spirituality" and human experience. What a bitter pill God's training must be to someone brought up in this spoon-fed generation!

> *"Trouble is training."*

Per the Scripture above, it is wrong to respond to hardship by taking it lightly (as some are prone to do) or by becoming discouraged (as others are prone to do). Instead, the Scriptures

213

teach that we need to be reassured by the fact that we are being treated as sons and daughters by our Father and being prepared for a *"harvest of righteousness and peace,"* if we learn our lessons from painful hardship.

This Scripture approaches the same subject matter from a slightly different angle:

> *Consider it pure joy, my brothers and sisters, whenever you face trials of many kinds, because you know that the testing of your faith produces perseverance. Let perseverance finish its work so that you may be mature and complete, not lacking anything. If any of you lacks wisdom, you should ask God, who gives generously to all without finding fault, and it will be given to you. But when you ask, you must believe and not doubt, because the one who doubts is like a wave of the sea, blown and tossed by the wind. That person should not expect to receive anything from the Lord. Such a person is double-minded and unstable in all they do.* (James 1:2-8)

We need to train ourselves to find joy, curiosity and fascination in our difficult trials. We must learn to enjoy the difficult work of the ministry and allow our perseverance to be strengthened so God can train us to maturity. There is always a battle to be had and true leaders savor the battle.

One of the tests of ministry is to profoundly appreciate the wounds of discipling. *"Wounds from a friend can be trusted, but an enemy multiplies kisses."* (Proverbs 27:6) As we "rise up" in leadership we come under scrutiny by more and more people. The result is painful wounds that can be trusted. This is the true "pay check" of ministry. We will grow from discipling; however, if one runs from this pain one will never grow. If one embraces it and seeks after it there is no way to stop such a person.

The author's second son David Kernan has the right attitude!

"But even if you should suffer for what is right, you are blessed." (1 Peter 3:14) The truth of the matter is, even when we have the "right" plan and we are doing things "right," there is still a "grindiness" to ministry that is bruising. In ministry, there is discomfort, heat and pressure, even when we are successful. There is no such thing as "painless" ministry-building. As Evan Bartholomew said, "Pressure makes diamonds out of coal." It is this grind that takes so many would-be ministers out - yet reveals the diamonds in others. We must embrace all our painful and sometimes insidious challenges as opportunities to draw closer to God and to learn from His Word. We must not have a mindset of loving the victory, the comfort and the glory, but rather to seek the rough and rugged work of the ministry - the "battle."

We ought always to thank God for you, brothers and sisters, and rightly so, because your faith is growing more and more, and the love all of you have for one another is increasing. Therefore, among God's churches we boast about your perseverance and faith in all the persecutions and trials you are enduring.

All this is evidence that God's judgment is right, and as a result you will be counted worthy of the Kingdom of God, for which you are suffering. God is just: He will pay back trouble to those who trouble you and give relief to you who are troubled, and to us as well. This will happen when the Lord Jesus is revealed from Heaven in blazing fire with His powerful angels. He will punish those who do not know God and do not obey the Gospel of our Lord Jesus. (2 Thessalonians 1:3-8)

In this incredible Scripture, we come to understand how true disciples handle *"persecutions and trials."* They draw close to God and one another. The opposite is the "let us just get through this" mentality. To my shame, I have fallen victim to this too many times. It can be hard to "self-diagnose" how "close to God" we are. That being said, God will always give us clues if we are ready to see them. Here is a good Scripture to guide us:

Love is patient, love is kind. It does not envy, it does not boast, it is not proud. It does not dishonor others, it is not self-seeking, it is not easily angered, it keeps no record of wrongs. Love does not delight in evil but rejoices with the truth. It always protects, always trusts, always hopes, always perseveres. Love never fails. (1 Corinthians 13:4-8)

If we are close to God in our trials, then our name should fit in these spaces,

(Tim) is patient, _____ is kind. _____ does not envy, _____ does not boast, _____ is not proud. _____ does not dishonor others, _____ is not self-seeking, _____ is not easily angered, _____ keeps no record of wrongs. _____ does not delight in evil but rejoices with the truth. _____ always protects, _____ always

trusts, _____ always hopes, _____ always perseveres. _____ never fails. (1 Corinthians 13:4-8)

Sometimes to gain power in our ministry, we must remember the axiom, "slow is smooth - smooth is fast." Rushing through your quiet times, being distracted in your interactions with others, failing to reach out to the lost, becoming exasperated and angry when faced with unexpected trials, all in the name of "pushing through" should give us a red alert. On the other hand, having great times God, caring about people, loving the lost, seeing God's hand in the twists and turns of the ministry (Romans 8:28), takes a little more time, but like a slow moving tsunami will sweep up everything in its wake.

Not only must we embrace the pressure with God, we must share the pressure. No one can carry the cross alone. *"As they were going out, they met a man from Cyrene, named Simon, and they forced him to carry the cross."* (Matthew 27:32) If we have a goal then distribute it among your small group leaders. If we have a problem share the load. We must not take the needs of the church upon ourselves alone. If we were to lie down on one nail what happens? We would be seriously injured! If we were to lie down on thousands of tightly packed nails what happens? It's a massage! Always share the pressure so that we and the whole church can succeed together!

Unlike the world with its pursuits, we are following a God who suffered many major losses during His faultless ministry. (John 6:66) We are imitating an Apostle, Paul, who was completely abandoned by his ministry in the last years of his life. (2 Timothy 1:15) These were gritty men. Why attach our joy and peace to what we cannot control? We must attach our joy and peace to our relationship with God. (Psalm 119:1-2)

The author at 17 years old being trained by God for the spiritual battles ahead.

Sadly, many leaders can fall into the temptation to pray for all their problems to be taken away. They do not realize that they simply do not want to need God. (1 Thessalonians 1:2; 3:10; 5:16-18) Challenges and trouble are God's plan to rehabilitate and train us as His disciples. A leader must instinctively understand suffering and be able to surmount disorientation, fatigue, defeat and pressure. Enjoy thinking about the problem, asking questions, and seeking insight. In a crisis, we need to be agents of God and be decisive.

Difficulty also provides an opportunity for disciples to band together! We can *"...carry each other's burdens, and in this way... fulfill the law of Christ."* (Galatians 6:2) Some of my most cherished memories are how friendship eased the pain of difficulty! Oftentimes, we would not have gone to one another for help without the difficulty in the first place!

> *These are the nations the Lord left to test all those Israelites who had not experienced any of the wars in Canaan (He did this only to teach warfare to the descendants of the Israelites who had not had previous battle experience): the five rulers of the Philistines, all the Canaanites, the Sidonians, and the Hivites living in the Lebanon mountains from Mount Baal Hermon to Lebo Hamath. They were left to test the Israelites to see whether they would obey the Lord's commands,*

which He had given their ancestors through Moses.
(Judges 3:1-4)

God using battle to train His people is not a new thing. As we see in this Scripture, God has always allowed adversity to test and prepare His people. Do not be surprised when God brings battle into our lives to give us seasoning and experience!

It is in times of great difficulty that we take comfort in the promises of God! *"And we know that in all things God works for the good of those who love Him, who have been called according to His purpose."* (Romans 8:28) There have been many times that I have had to repeat that Scripture in my mind every five minutes. Sometimes the "train wreck" is God taking a grip on the ministry, pruning and preparing us for the next level!

Timothy David Kernan Jr. is eager for the fight!

What if every disciple had this attitude and these convictions towards the battles we face in world evangelism? Far fewer people would give up! Far fewer people would become discouraged and quit! It is not without reason that the Bible warns in Job 36:21, *"Beware of turning to evil, which you seem to prefer to affliction."* There is a terrible lack of plain, old-fashioned intestinal fortitude in this world. Sadly, this insecurity and fear can sometimes even make its way into the fellowship.

One of the "battles" of ministry is coping with fatigue. I love Jason Dimitry's quote, "Exhaustion is a symptom of being a sold-out disciple." A committed disciple is always pushing themselves, and yet God continues to give them the strength to make it the next mile. ***"He gives strength to the weary and increases the power of the weak."*** (Isaiah 40:2)

"Loving the battle" comes down to being more attached to our values than we are to the outward circumstances that exist and to what Satan is throwing at us at any given moment in time. When someone is "loving the battle" and everything is stripped away, they can still say, ***"And now these three remain: faith, hope and love. But the greatest of these is love."*** (1 Corinthians 13:13) It is about being fixed on our faith and not our difficulties or our bills or how those around us are "doing." It is about staying in the game when we are betrayed, suspected, distrusted, abandoned or mocked. (1 Timothy 6:4) It is about cherishing and extending forgiveness and that special hope in the resurrection that only Christ can provide. It is about refusing to let our love grow cold even if the price is our life. (Matthew 24:12)

The Kingdom of God does not need oversensitive men. It needs considerate and compassionate men who can fight lions. Rest assured, there is no alternative to "loving the battle." Problems multiply and expand when we avoid and take shortcuts to get out of difficulty. We need to go to God and then engage. Is it not better to die fighting than to die worrying? If anyone doubts that trouble and even death are part of the Christian walk, then let us simply consider the deaths of some of the early church leaders:

Reliable tradition has it that Matthew was killed in Ethiopia by a sword wound. Mark was dragged to death behind horses in the streets of Alexandria. Luke was hung. John was boiled in oil but survived to be the only Apostle to die of old age. Peter was crucified upside down. James the Just was thrown off the temple roof and then clubbed to death. James the Greater was beheaded.

Bartholomew was skinned to death by a whip. Andrew preached for two days from the cross where he was crucified and finally died. Thomas was stabbed in the back with a spear in India. Jude was shot with arrows. Mathias was stoned and then beheaded. Barnabas was stoned. Paul was beheaded. This is clear evidence that all of God's beloved servants endured horrific trials.

This is a prayer from a British SAS commando, Lt. Andre Zirnheld, who died in battle July 26, 1941. The following was found in his uniform:

I bring this prayer to You, Lord
For You alone can give
What one cannot demand from oneself.
Give me, Lord, what You have left over,
Give me what no one ever asks You for.
I don't ask You for rest, or quiet,
Whether of soul or body;
I don't ask You for wealth,
Nor for success, nor even health perhaps.
That sort of thing You get asked for so much
That You can't have any of it left.
Give me, Lord, what You have left over,
Give me what no-one wants from You.
I want insecurity, strife,
And I want You to give me these
Once and for all.
So that I can be sure of having them always,
Since I shall not always have the courage
To ask You for them.
Give me, Lord, what You have left over,
Give me what others want nothing to do with.
But give me courage too,
And strength and faith;

For You alone can give
What one cannot demand from oneself.

What an incredible example of loving the battle! This reminds me of Romans 5:3-5:

> *Not only so, but we also glory in our sufferings, because we know that suffering produces perseverance; perseverance, character; and character, hope. And hope does not put us to shame, because God's love has been poured out into our hearts through the Holy Spirit, who has been given to us.*

Cory and Jee Blackwell (right) - the Chicago International Christian Church Leaders - are best of friends with RD and April Baker, the courageous Dubai International Christian Church Leaders.

What if every disciple had this same perspective? As my dear brother Blaise Feumba exhorts, "Seek His presence more than His presents." Sometimes God puts problems in our life so we can fight them and overcome them together! By wishing they would go away, we miss the most life-changing and character-refining lessons!

Practically speaking, regarding grand strokes, do we have actual plans for modern-day challenges? For instance, if we live in an earthquake, hurricane, or tsunami zone, have we sat down with our leaders to discuss what our ministry might do in the event of a disaster like that? For example, in California, we are concerned about earthquakes, and every House Church Leadership Couple in the CAICC have a plan to take care of the needs of the members of the Bible Talks they oversee. The church is responsible for the souls of the disciples and should plan for any contingency. Even if a disaster never strikes, we would have to believe that having a plan would bring quite a bit of security and a mindset of preparedness to the church!

Do we have a daunting financial goal to hit during a fundraiser? For some, this feels like a battle! Consider a "Christian fundraiser" course. Teach on fundraising, assign books, bring in guest speakers. What will the final exam be? The fundraiser itself! However, in the meantime, we have turned a difficult challenge into a strengthening exercise.

Having trouble with religious groups and persecution on campus? What would Jesus do? Organize a debate! We can invite all our persecutors to a room that we have booked and have a discussion on the Bible. (Acts 9:29) When they see our earnestness and Biblical convictions, who knows if some might join us? We can turn problems into opportunities!

For whatever problem, we need to always find instances where other ministers have overcome and create "case studies" from which our people can learn. As the leader, our job is to not just be the preacher of the Gospel, but the preacher of the Gospel to every situation. We need to be "solution evangelists" - the problem-solvers of our ministries. This is a big piece of how we fight! As Paul wrote, *"I want to know Christ - yes, to know the power of His resurrection and participation in His sufferings, becoming like Him in His death."* (Philippians 3:10) We need to teach people in the church how to struggle! So many need to build conviction on this. It is not without reason that Jesus taught, *"Whoever does not take up their cross and follow me is not worthy of me."* (Matthew 10:38)

A couple who truly loves the battle, Mark and Kerri Garrido, are the hard-fighting soldiers of the Lord and leaders of the Hawaiian Islands!

How we take the beatings that inevitably come in the ministry defines us as leaders and can be God's way of proving our faith and challenging others. *"For it has been granted to you on behalf of Christ not only to believe in Him, but also to suffer for Him."* (Philippians 1:29) Sometimes the best strategy is simply to face our problems, get advice, seek relevant Scriptures, get close to God, and hack at the problem until it is resolved, be it a long battle or a short one. As Jesus said, *"To Him who overcomes, I will give the right to sit with me on my throne, just as I overcame and sat down with my Father on his throne."* (Revelations 3:21) It is about getting connected to our God and engaging what is happening around us.

The amazing thing about loving the battle - and not shirking the sufferings of Christ - is that when we do so, we also get the comfort of Christ. *"Praise be to the God and Father of our Lord Jesus Christ, the Father of compassion and the God of all comfort, who comforts us in all our troubles, so that we can comfort those in any trouble with the comfort we ourselves receive from God. For just as we share abundantly in the sufferings of Christ, so also our comfort abounds through Christ."* (2 Corinthians 1:3-5) Let us steadily advance forward into the battle ahead!

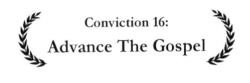

Conviction 16:
Advance The Gospel

Only one message can change the world. Deliver it!

**Kip McKean serving the poor at Smokey Mountain
in Manila, Philippines in 1989.**

*Fellow Israelites, listen to this: Jesus of Nazareth was
a man accredited by God to you by miracles, wonders
and signs, which God did among you through Him, as
you yourselves know. This man was handed over to*

you by God's deliberate plan and foreknowledge; and you, with the help of wicked men, put Him to death by nailing Him to the cross. But God raised Him from the dead, freeing Him from the agony of death, because it was impossible for death to keep its hold on Him. (Acts 2:22-24)

What an incredible message! It is the Gospel! Jesus is the Son of God; died on the cross for the forgiveness of our sins; was resurrected from the dead; and is now seated at the right hand of the Father! The news of this message is simple enough to be spread between prison bars, from one friend to another, or even between strangers. There is no one on Earth - from the elite living in the highest echelons of society to the homeless living on garbage dumps in the third world - to whom this message is not relevant and urgent.

If we wanted to make a movie about it, we would need to capture God's eternal nature and limitless power. We would need to visualize His endless generosity in creating the universe and the world. We would need to find a way to put on the screen His vulnerability to us and the pain He felt as we chose sin instead of life with Him in eternity. Then, somehow, we would need to describe on film the miracle of His victorious plan to retrieve us and bring us back into His presence.

The movie would have to bring out the wonder of the Old Testament and then make us fall in love with Jesus, His very presence on earth. It would need to cut our hearts at the image of Jesus' shattered body approaching the cross. The movie would need to end with the audience looking at themselves. It would be quite a film, if it could somehow scratch the surface of how amazing the Gospel is. The Gospel, which means "good news" in Greek, is the explanation of the universe. It is still our message today.

Sadly, many Christians are no longer captivated by the Gospel. The reality is that the three elements of the Gospel - Jesus's crucifixion, resurrection and ascension - have become obscure and boring to many. Some so-called "Christians" cannot even tell us what the Gospel is... What a shame!

The Scriptures are so rich with the Gospel. As leaders in the Kingdom of God, we must not fail to bring home its might. Acts 14:19-21 so powerfully describes the ferocious zeal of the Apostles to preach the Gospel, *"Then some Jews came from Antioch and Iconium and won the crowd over. They stoned Paul and dragged him outside the city, thinking he was dead. But after the disciples had gathered around him, he got up and went back into the city. The next day he and Barnabas left for Derbe. They preached the Gospel in that city and won a large number of disciples."* What an incredible passage! Disciples were (and still are) won from preaching the Gospel, and there was nothing that would hold back Paul and Barnabas from preaching it!

Paul's writings are full of his passion for the Gospel. Let us take a quick tour of the Gospel in Paul's writings. In Romans 1:16, Paul declares, *"For I am not ashamed of the Gospel, because it is the power of God that brings salvation to everyone who believes..."* In Romans 15:20 he proclaims, *"It has always been my ambition to preach the Gospel where Christ was not known..."* In 1 Corinthians 9:16 he writes, *"For when I preach the Gospel, I cannot boast, since I am compelled to preach. Woe to me if I do not preach the Gospel!"* In 1 Corinthians 15:1-2 the Bible states, *"Now, brothers and sisters, I want to remind you of the Gospel I preached to you, which you received and on which you have taken your stand. By this Gospel you are saved, if you hold firmly to the Word I preached to you. Otherwise, you have believed in vain."* There is little doubt about the role and prominence of the Gospel in the ministry of Paul.

In Ephesians 6:19, Paul requests that the disciples, *"Pray also for me, that whenever I speak, words may be given me so that I will fearlessly make known the mystery of the Gospel."* When Paul is persecuted and unjustly arrested, he writes to the Philippians in 1:14, *"And because of my chains, most of the brothers and sisters have become confident in the Lord and dare all the more to proclaim the Gospel without fear."* His only concern for the disciples is that, *"whatever happens, conduct yourselves in a manner worthy of the Gospel of Christ. Then, whether I come and see you or only hear about you in my absence, I will know that you stand firm in the one Spirit, striving together as one for the faith of the Gospel."* (Philippians 1:27)

Paul's dream was coming true because *"...the Gospel is bearing fruit and growing throughout the whole world - just as it has been doing among you since the day you heard it and truly understood God's grace."* (Colossians 1:6) Nevertheless, he warns in 2 Thessalonians 1:8, *"He will punish those who do not know God and do not obey the Gospel of our Lord Jesus."*

> *"Human history has repeatedly demonstrated that an idea, at the right time and place, is more powerful than anything!"*

How important was the Gospel in the life of the first-century church? It was their life. It was their message. It was how they advanced. When people heard and were cut to the heart, the family grew! In many ways, we make life a lot harder for ourselves in this century than our first-century brothers and sisters did. We put emphasis on what we think attracts people rather than what cures them.

Human history has repeatedly demonstrated that an idea, at the right time and place, is more powerful than anything! No one can win a fight against an idea with violence. We can only win with an improved idea - better realized. This is a powerful truth. We have seen ideas create movements time and time again. They have changed the world, for better or worse, with devastating force. Examples abound: the Anti-Apartheid Movement, the anti-war movements, the Civil Rights Movement, the Environmental Movement, the Feminist Movement, the Human Rights Movement, the Labor Movement, Communism, the Occupy Movement, the Prohibition Movement, Right To Life Movement, and the Women's Suffrage Movement. For good or for evil, when a message comes and gains traction in the hearts and minds of people, anything is possible. Yet, every movement of human origin has led to excesses, abuses and re-enslavement. Only the Gospel is the ultimate answer to the problems of mankind.

The Gospel is a message about respect for life. It is a message about dignity and freedom. It reaches men and women as equals, yet protects their differences and strengthens their relationships. It reaches all races and all nations and calls them together into the same Kingdom. It calls us to drop our weapons and pick up pruning hooks to reap a harvest. It protects the poor, gives generously, and frees the captive. It is a conquering force that wills to occupy every campus and every neighborhood! As stated before, the Gospel is relevant on the mean streets, the main streets, the moneyed streets and every other street! It is a movement of workers who seek to labor for the Lord. It is a movement of love that seeks to light the darkness of a polluted, addicted, lonely, impoverished and suffering world. How relevant is the Gospel today? Its importance surpasses every movement in history.

The American revolutionary Samuel Adams once said, "It does not take a majority to prevail... but rather an irate, tireless minority, keen on setting brushfires of freedom in people's minds." His words ring very true. There must be a small vanguard of revolutionaries spreading the powerful Gospel until it becomes a raging fire.

Why try to attract people to church through worldly means when we can instead teach them the Gospel, and in that sense, bring the church to them! The best way to make a leader is to give them the healing message that comes from the Gospel and teaching them to become healers as well.

The first universities were dedicated to the study of the Gospel. Sadly, today the corporate world has its influence so deep in our college campuses that, from their first year of study, students are being trained for a job position rather than being trained to think about life and the world. When asked what the purpose of life is, campus students - the most privileged people on the earth and the most capable of changing it - often list "enjoying pleasure." The Gospel needs to reconquer the campuses of this dark world.

We cannot advance our ministry, make a disciple, or raise someone up as a leader without advancing the Gospel. It is by impacting the lost with the Gospel and teaching the Gospel to the disciples that we make disciples and leaders. Sometimes the ministry can feel so complex and overwhelming. It can start to feel hard to convince someone to join the church or be a disciple. However, if we can convince them of the truth of the Gospel, then the rest falls into place automatically. Believe in the power of our message! Let us "occupy" the minds of those around us with the Gospel!

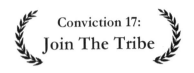

Conviction 17:
Join The Tribe

The first-century church was a tribe in a tribal world... Now is the time to resurrect the tribe in your ministry!

The author was very proud of how the Armor Bearers surrounded Kenneth Woods at his mother's funeral.

While Jesus was still talking to the crowd, someone told Him, "Your mother and brothers are standing outside, wanting to speak to you." He replied to him, "Who is my mother, and who are my brothers?"

Pointing to His disciples, He said, "Here are my mother and my brothers. For whoever does the will of my Father in Heaven is my brother and sister and mother. (Matthew 12:46-50)

In this passage, Jesus reveals for us the incredible nature of the church. Our obedience to God's will grants us access to the family of Christ. That membership brings us many spiritual sons and daughters, sisters, brothers, mothers and fathers.

Joel and Courtney Parlour, dear friends and family!

Today, so many people - both young and old - seek this feeling of family and belonging. However, Satan is there to help "meet" this need through violent gangs on the streets and immoral "fraternities" on college campuses, to name a few. He stands ready to work with the loneliness people feel to ensnare them in so many ways. On the other hand, God has provided the church, the body of Christ, to provide a true family for all mankind.

As in Biblical times, today, many of the world's people (outside the first world) are born into and die as part of a tribe. Why?

With a high unemployment rate in the "undeveloped" world, people need to belong to a tribe to survive. The simple rationale and attractiveness of the concept of the tribe is that our problems are no longer ours alone. Instead, they become the problems of the entire tribe and vice versa. The logic plays out every day. For example, if one person has a job only one week out of four, that person would be happy to push his earnings towards the leadership of the tribe, because during the weeks when he is not earning, he and his family would be supported by the tribe. Also, in countries with little public security, the tribe provides protection from threats. People know that in a tribe, they will never be abandoned or alone.

By contrast, in the Western world, technological advancements and plentiful energy resources have skyrocketed the standard of living and wealth so that people no longer have the same immediate need for community. Simply put, they have wealth that they do not want to share. Literally, our social structure is breaking apart as it soars forcefully upward on an upsurge of wealth. This lack of a feeling of need for one another, due to self-sufficiency, has sinfully broken up the family unit and turned the clear majority of churches into entertainment venues instead of close-knit families.

In addition, the more society's families are broken up by easy divorce, single parenthood, fatherless children, homosexuality, etc., the more people must work, pay taxes, and be consumers instead of serving in the home. Therefore, individualism and consumerism provides a "high" to an economy, but has detrimental long-term effects on the people. The "hangover" of this high is brutal. The

> "*Today in the Western world, the new religion of state is what I call 'The Cult of The Individual.'*"

stresses of being alone have led to a surge in depression, anxiety, drug use - both prescribed and illegal - alcoholism and even suicide. Today, in the Western world, the new religion of state is what I call, "The Cult of The Individual." Sadly, people are terrified of anything that contradicts radical individualism. We have entered a time of conformity to individualism - ironic as that is - which is completely at odds with the teachings of the Gospel.

Imagine the Gospel as a meteorite entering the atmosphere of the modern world. As it descends with great speed towards the earth, there is friction with the air that creates a ball of flame around it. That flaming area of friction between the Gospel and the world is what we call ministry. The flaming tip of the meteorite, the very hottest part right at the forefront, is the topic of discipleship, discipling and the role of the church as a real family of God.

Let us get our footing in the Old Testament, then move into the New Testament to see if we can grasp what kind of family we are supposed to be as the church.

> **Abraham will surely become a great and powerful nation, and all nations on earth will be blessed through him. For I have chosen him, so that he will direct his children and his household after him to keep the way of the Lord by doing what is right and just, so that the Lord will bring about for Abraham what He has promised him.** (Genesis 18:18-19)

In the Old Testament, it was Abraham's family that would become God's "chosen people." From the very beginning, as we see in this

235

passage, God expected His tribe to stay faithful to His instructions and obey Him from generation to generation. Anyone with a knowledge of the Old Testament knows that Israel was a tribal community. How did someone become a part of the House of Israel in Old Testament times? They were born into it or adopted into it! In the New Testament, membership in the tribe is the same! Let us look at this passage,

> *Therefore, remember that formerly you who are Gentiles by birth and called "uncircumcised" by those who call themselves "the circumcision" (that done in the body by the hands of men) - remember that at that time you were separate from Christ, excluded from citizenship in Israel and foreigners to the covenants of the promise, without hope and without God in the world. But now, in Christ Jesus, you who once were far away have been brought near through the blood of Christ...*
>
> *Consequently, you are no longer foreigners and aliens, but fellow citizens with God's people and members of God's household, built on the foundation of the Apostles and prophets, with Christ Jesus Himself as the chief cornerstone.* (Ephesians 2:11-22 Abridged)

This is an incredible passage that clearly shows the church to be God's family in the first century. A beautiful, descriptive passage that further demonstrates the point is Acts 4:32-35:

> *All the believers were one in heart and mind. No one claimed that any of their possessions was their own, but they shared everything they had. With great power, the Apostles continued to testify to the resurrection of the Lord Jesus. And God's grace was so powerfully at*

work in them all that there were no needy persons among them. For from time to time those who owned land or houses sold them, brought the money from the sales and put it at the Apostles' feet, and it was distributed to anyone who had need.

Ryan Keenan - a dear old friend of the author - is the trusted Administrator for the Tribe World Sector.

This is a remarkable Scripture that shows the life and mindset of the disciples in the church! It is not a prescription for how the church should be, but rather this is a description of how it was! The disciples were *"unified in heart and mind."* Just as a man today does not consider that his possessions belong only to himself, but to his wife and children as well, the first-century church considered that everything belonged to their church family! This was a true tribe!

Every disciple - and all the more, every leader in the church - needs to understand what belonging to the tribe means. What bonded them together so strongly? Today, what bonds people together is ethnicity, skin color, common interests and work relationships. Nevertheless, the first-century church was not bonded together on such weak and trivial grounds. The first-century church was bonded on the redeeming blood of Christ Jesus, a common commitment and the hope in the resurrection. (Acts 4:33)

Disciples in the first century were described by Peter as *"…a chosen people, a royal priesthood, a holy nation, God's special possession, that you may declare the praises of Him who called you out of darkness into His wonderful light. Once you were not a people, but now you are the people of God; once you had not received mercy, but now you have received mercy."* (1 Peter 2:9-10) A people, a priesthood, a nation: these are powerful words that describe what we are to God. We are not mere "church service attenders," but a family!

Caleb and Lizbeth Cohen: A powerful Evangelist and Women's Ministry Leader couple!

It is hard for modern people from first world countries to understand that Christianity is not merely an ideology or philosophy, but instead a family and tribe in which we are graciously given membership by God Himself. For many, the atomizing individualism of our society creates a mental barrier preventing us from grasping the "tribe" or family concept. This is simply because most of us today do not come from tribes, strong families, or even strong friendships anymore.

Many of us come from broken homes - homes with workaholics, abuse, addiction, divorce and selfishness. Thus, we do not have the skills to work with others or to be accountable to others as part of a true family. The "tribal" family nature of the church - woven throughout the Bible and fully embraced by its writers - is foreign to us.

If we do not understand the church of the New Testament, then as we read the Scriptures, we involuntarily superimpose our worldview onto the Bible instead of learning from the Bible. It is important to slip into our "Bible times" sandals and read the Scriptures with humility, deductively trying to understand, instead of inductively imposing our biased views onto the Scriptures.

I am eternally grateful to God that He revealed this to me when I became a Christian sixteen years ago. By God's mercy, I could see both the struggling campus students around me as the "holy saints" they were and our little church - meeting in a high school gymnasium - as a *"royal priesthood."* Yet, I will never forget the moment that the true grandeur and power of the church, Jesus' body on earth, struck me; it was at the 2001 Pass The Torch Conference in Toronto, Canada. There were thousands of disciples in a massive conference room with all the lights turned off, except for the torches that surrounded the choir in the front as we sang. My heart sang for me because my mouth was busy crying as I comprehended the majesty and mercy of God's Kingdom. My heart was filled with joy that day and I have never forgotten that glorious image that was burned into my mind of what the church should be. Yet, I still did not fully understand "the tribe."

I have been immensely blessed by a half dozen trips to Africa, in particular, the Democratic Republic of Congo. It was in 2006, in planting a small church there, that I first came to understand "tribe." In the first days of our interactions, the disciples there were amazed by my cell phone and camera. However, when I left, they were not crying that I was taking away my technology. I was crying because I had never felt so adopted and pulled into an extended family. Through my trips to Congo, Kenya and Ethiopia, I was able to experience first-hand churches that were nestled into tribal societies. So much of the Bible was opened to me because of these experiences.

Today, many fall away from the faith because they struggle to operate as part of a family and retreat to familiar self-reliance and worldly individualism. Even strong disciples struggle with submitting to the authority in the church, because on some level, they still have one foot in the world. When we with our individual spirit come into a close-knit church - that holds to the model of the first-century church and practice spiritual accountability - it can be very hard to adapt. It is predictable that our spiritual immaturity will blossom into distrust, selfish ambition, lies, feelings of insecurity and pride. Just as feral cats fight being tamed (have you ever tried to lead a "herd" of cats?), we as individualistic people find it hard to be brought into a family where we can be nurtured and protected.

Because of today's broken society, we face a problem that the first-century church did not face as intensely. In the first-century church, the level of accountability, "teach-ability" and structure naturally existed because the church was filled with converts from a strong tribal milieu - the various Mediterranean cultures. We do not have that advantage today. The solution? Well, the process begins even before baptism. We must apply the Bible - both relevant Old and New Testament Scriptures - through formal, caring "discipling" and Bible Talk families. These basics of tribal culture need to be lovingly taught to every new convert. Then at baptism we appoint the new convert a "discipler" (a spiritual mentor) and place them in a "Bible Talk" - a small group with members, visonary leadership, a geographic charge and an awesome name. For many, this very well might be the first time they have ever been part of a family!

It is easy for us, especially as leaders, to become impatient and "write people off" as "obstinate" and "prideful." While that may be true, it is better to say, "I have failed to win them over." I have found that if I take the time to teach new converts about the "tribe" they have come into as disciples, their defensiveness melts away. Those who come from broken families may struggle to understand how good it is to belong to a spiritual family. This is where we, as leaders and shepherds, need to devote special attention.

**The Tribe World Sector wristbands remind
us daily that we are friends and
partners forever!**

As my dear brother Cory Blackwell always says, "Love God, love people." So much of ministry can be broken down into that simple phrase! As people struggle with being part of a family, mantra needs to be constantly brought to the forefront.

As leaders, we need to be an example and lead with moral authority. If we cannot submit to those *"over us in the Lord"* (1 Thessalonians 5:12), we will make it difficult for those under us who have no model to imitate. Let us be the examples to our flock so we can help our more independent siblings to "come in from the cold."

> *Jesus went through all the towns and villages, teaching in their synagogues, proclaiming the good news of the Kingdom and healing every disease and sickness. When He saw the crowds, He had compassion on them, because they were harassed and helpless, like sheep without a shepherd. Then He said to His disciples, "The harvest is plentiful but the workers are few. Ask the Lord of the harvest, therefore, to send out workers into His harvest field." Jesus called His twelve disciples to Him and gave them authority to drive out impure spirits and to heal every disease and sickness.* (Matthew 9:35-10:1)

Some might argue that the term "discipling" does not come up in the Bible and that nowhere do we see a system of appointing discipling partners and creating "discipling trees" in churches. This observation is only partially true. Those who too enthusiastically advance this observation must not lose sight of the forest for the "d-trees." When Jesus saw the *"harassed and helpless"* people, He had compassion on them because they were *"like sheep without a shepherd."* The solution Jesus was advocating was that they would be given shepherds and leaders. While we do not see the word "discipling" in the Bible, we see that this is God's plan for mankind; we see discipling in practice.

Conversely, what we do not see in the New Testament Church (that we see in the world today) is a pack of wild, autonomous individuals who lack the cohesion to organize a picnic, let alone the evangelization of the world. Discipling relationships recreate the dynamic partnerships that form a healthy "church tribe." Discipling is a methodology of God, and God's forceful leaders have always implemented "methodology" to achieve obedience to His will. The "tribe of God" is desperately needed in this lonely world.

The visit to the Congo in 2006 was the inspiration for the name of the author's World Sector - The Tribe.

The family is one of the most attractive things about the church. People have an immediate positive, emotional reaction when they come to our meetings because they see the love of the family of God! (John 13:34-35) It satisfies a deep inner need that has been put there by God. Let us resurrect the tribe in the church and usher in a time of powerful growth simply by letting the church be what it is - God's family on earth!

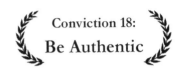

Conviction 18:
Be Authentic

"Wholesome," "fresh," "real," "good," "pure," "all-natural,"
"original," "authentic," "simple," "true," "classic" and
"time-honored." These are words the world uses to
sell potato chips. Why? Because advertiser know
that people crave the authentic. Here is how
to re-own authenticity in our ministry.

**The brothers in Chennai, India are
having a blast playing volleyball!**

Finally, brothers, whatever is true, whatever is noble, whatever is right, whatever is pure, whatever is lovely, whatever is admirable - if anything is excellent or praiseworthy - think about such things. (Philippians 4:8)

The Kingdom of God is not about tele-evangelism, game-show hosting, radio shows or even massive concert-style Sunday services. The Kingdom of God is about truth, nobility, righteousness, purity, beauty and honor. It is not about what is outside, but what is inside. (Luke 17:21)

Lianne Kernan - the authors beautiful wife - visiting Northern India.

That said, the world can start to creep into the church and authenticity can be lost. Hype can replace proclamation; popularity can supplant honor; pleasure can supersede responsibility; and the pretend can displace the authentic. The fellowship can become the entertainment business or even the therapist's office, and evangelism can become the sales room. People can begin to use people and love things instead of loving people and using things.

"Wholesome," "fresh," "real," "good," "pure," "all-natural," "original," "authentic," "simple," "true," "classic" and "time-honored" are but some of the words advertising companies use to make people snatch products off the shelf. In fact, it is hard to find a product that does not have a couple of these words on it. Why? Because the advertising gurus of the world discovered that "authenticity" is one of the concepts that draws people's attention and sells a product, even more than sex and insecurity.

The commercial world has caught on to the thirst of human beings for the authentic and is making trillions of dollars (no exaggeration) with it. People may buy an item because they believe as they are told, that the product will make them "happy," protect them from embarrassment, or make them attractive to the opposite sex. However, tell them that something is "authentic," "wholesome" and "true," and they will buy just about anything. Indeed, some people subscribe many modern movements to the thirst for authenticity and a revulsion of the constant stream of impurity, insecurity, rebellion and materialism that passes for modern Western culture.

> *"One could explain the rise of modern Islam with a thirst for authenticity."*

One could explain the rise of modern Islam with a thirst for authenticity. The father of modern Sunni Islam and the Islamic Brotherhood Movement, Sayyid Qutb, was a student in the United States during the 1950's, a period most North Americans consider a conservative era. Mr. Qutb observed a dangerous culture of excessive disrespect for authority and pleasure-seeking. Most do not associate the 1950's with these ideas, but that was his perspective. He returned to his native Egypt devoted and determined to prevent "Westernism" from getting a foothold on his shores. He wrote the now-famous book *Ma'alim fi-l-Tariq (Milestones)* and became the "Karl Marx" of modern Islam. His writings reignited a feeling of authenticity and purity that people could experience through Islam. His message of clean living, mixed with hatred and disgust for the Western world, has resonated with millions of people and spread from Eastern China to the shores of the Western Sahara. The rise of Wahhabist, (conservative Sunni Islam) Takfirist (believing that all Muslims who do not agree are not Muslims) Islam is one of the most powerful resurgences in modern history.

While Islam has been thriving in prisons and among the poor, even major fast-food chains have found new life through "authenticity." One famous restaurant chain, McDonalds, came back from the brink of bankruptcy by selling "wholesome, fresh, real, pure oatmeal, side-salad goodness, and 100% real beef." Indeed, a walk through any supermarket will clearly illustrate the very aggressive use of "authentic" advertising to sell goods to a market hungry for "the real thing."

On college campuses, Islam, but also Wicca and Paganism, are getting traction with young people who want to know what is "real." On the other hand, Christianity, the most legitimate and pure establishment to ever set foot on God's green Earth, is branded by popular culture as "unhealthy, stale, fake, hypocritical, tainted, contrived, fraudulent, complicated, false, weird, hateful and disposable." Only Satan could pull off such an effective job of slandering the truth.

Worse, how does modern "Christianity" respond? By apologizing, liberalizing the message, "gimmick-izing" the church, and turning leaders into "worship experience coordinators" who come off sounding like door-to-door salesmen. Enough is enough! It is time for the church to get back to its roots and put an end to being defined by our enemies. We are God's people; God's family! There is nothing purer and more authentic than that, and we must own it! There have been many failed "authenticity movements" in denominational Christianity. Sadly, all have failed because they were about cleaning the outside of the cup and not the inside. (Luke 11:39) Bringing guitars to church, having the mass in the local language, in a home or cross-legged in the park is not going to suddenly make the church more authentic.

True authenticity is not about a time-honored recipe for potato chips or pie. Authenticity is about watching *"your life and doctrine closely."* (1 Timothy 4:16) It is about how we live and what we value. It is about the painful process of keeping those two things together and being open when we fail.

> *This is the message we have heard from Him and declare to you: God is light; in Him there is no darkness at all. If we claim to have fellowship with Him yet walk in the darkness, we lie and do not live by the truth. But if we walk in the light, as He is in the light, we have fellowship with one another, and the blood of Jesus, His Son, purifies us from all sin.*
>
> *If we claim to be without sin, we deceive ourselves and the truth is not in us. If we confess our sins, He is faithful and just and will forgive us our sins and purify us from all unrighteousness. If we claim we have not sinned, we make Him out to be a liar and His Word has no place in our lives.* (1 John 1:5-10)

When people confess their sins to each other, look at what happens: They walk in the light, the truth is in them, and they are purified by the blood of Christ! What could be more authentic? Secondly, according to the Scripture, genuine friendships flourish and stale fakeness departs! At that point, it does not matter if there are guitars or where the meeting is being held, because authenticity would have been achieved through confession, repentance and trust.

My dear friend Michael Kirchner has been indispensable in building the administration in each of the SoldOut Movement Churches.

Confession is a powerful tool that brings trust, fellowship and unity. In a disunified situation, it is always good to create opportunities for openness. A "Night of Atonement" is a meeting where everyone comes together and confesses their sins to one another. This can be done in small groups - men and women separately - or as a congregation. If there are still any outstanding issues after a meeting like that, they can be addressed on a Matthew 18 basis. A powerful Night of Atonement can completely unify a ministry! Before having a "Night of Atonement," as done in Portland, it is good to get with people individually and confirm that everyone sees their own sin and is ready to be open and vulnerable.

One of the great times of the year for the City of Angeles International Christian Church Staff is when we go up into the San Bernardino Mountains to spend a weekend of bonding before we head out for Christmas holidays. The Overseeing Evangelists and Women's Ministry Leaders head up Sunday night. We make dinner together, and then everyone takes turns sharing their whole life story! It takes about 24 hours, but there are so many laughs and tears. The following day, the Region Leaders, Admins and Shepherds join us for a great meal followed by a massive group confession time. The sisters are in one room and the brothers in another. Before the confession time starts, the tension is so thick it could be cut with a knife. However, as one disciple after another shares their shortcomings - beginning with Lianne and I as the leaders - love and compassion enter and fill the room!

In 2 Timothy 2:22 Paul writes, ***"Flee the evil desires of youth, and pursue righteousness, faith, love and peace, along with those who call on the Lord out of a pure heart."*** Through openness, true leaders become best friends. Deep friendships create genuineness and openness in the ministry.

This is an important lesson, especially for young, capable and ambitious leaders. People do not just want what we can do for them or to know how capable we are. People want a piece of us and a real friendship with us. Let me rephrase this for emphasis: They do not want what we can do; they want us! We can win many battles in ministry on our talent and skill, but if we lose our spouses, our children, our friends and our peers, then we have lost the war! Take careful note of this.

Let us bring powerful authenticity into our ministry! Let us refresh our lives and doctrine and be open about when we need to repent and learn. Then we will hear the disciples say, "Our ministry is 'wholesome,' 'fresh,' 'real,' 'good,' 'pure,' 'all-natural,' 'original,' 'authentic,' 'simple,' 'true,' 'classic' and 'time-honored.'" This is not optional. It is what the church must be!

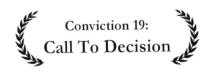

Conviction 19:
Call To Decision

Satan blurs the difference between good and evil. He clouds the decisive choices that lead to success. The path to victory is found by constantly calling everyone to radical decisions.

Matt and Helen Sullivan, a powerful church-building couple, have served in the Crossroads Movement, the International Churches of Christ and the International Christian Church. Their lives are a testimony to powerful decisions and the fruit they can bear.

See, I set before you today life and prosperity, death and destruction. For I command you today to love the Lord your God, to walk in His ways, and to keep His commands, decrees and laws; then you will live and increase, and the Lord your God will bless you in the land you are entering to possess.

But if your heart turns away and you are not obedient, and if you are drawn away to bow down to other gods and worship them, I declare to you this day that you will certainly be destroyed. You will not live long in the land you are crossing the Jordan to enter and possess.

This day I call Heaven and Earth as witnesses against you, that I have set before you life and death, blessings and curses. Now choose life, so that you and your children may live and that you may love the Lord your God, listen to His voice, and hold fast to Him.
(Deuteronomy 30: 15-20)

Here, Moses clearly defines the choices before God's people. He defines the difference between God and idols; then calls the people to a decision to follow God. Indeed, when we read about the visionary leadership of great men like Jesus, Moses and Paul, they constantly define the difference between God and the world.

Noam Chomsky, the American philosopher, once wrote, "As soon as questions of will or decision or reason or choice of action arise, human science is at a loss." That is because human decisions are inherently spiritual. The modern sciences and atheistic studies are of no use in this arena. As a minister calling people to liberating, spiritual decisions, we are the only ones capable of helping the people in this world. Prayerful and well thought-out tough decisions must become a calling card of our ministry. Jesus said,

If anyone comes to me and does not hate father and mother, wife and children, brothers and sisters - yes, even their own life - such a person cannot be my disciple. And whoever does not carry their cross and follow me cannot be my disciple.

Suppose one of you wants to build a tower. Won't you first sit down and estimate the cost to see if you have enough money to complete it? For if you lay the foundation and are not able to finish it, everyone who sees it will ridicule you, saying, "This person began to build and wasn't able to finish."

Or suppose a king is about to go to war against another king. Won't he first sit down and consider whether he is able with ten thousand men to oppose the one coming against Him with twenty thousand? If he is not able, he will send a delegation while the other is still a long way off and will ask for terms of peace. In the same way any of you who does not give up everything he has cannot be my disciple. (Luke 14:26-33)

Allow me to paraphrase this Scripture in modern parlance, "Following me is a hard decision. It is not one that should be made lightly. Before becoming a disciple, think hard, but think fast!" Jesus was all about calling people to decisive action for God. He was demanding and commanding in His life-giving call to discipleship.

Also, take note that He was talking to a large crowd who probably did not know Him very well. The idea that ministers need to have incredible personal relationships with those they challenge and that the recipients will always take those challenges well is both "unbiblical" and "un-Jesus-like." We must challenge everyone to make decisions for God.

Sometimes the reason we do not call our ministries to hard decisions is insecurity. Insecurity and the pride is produces can drive us to take an "I got this" approach to ministry instead of calling everyone to decisions and seeing how much their talents and sacrifice is needed. This is a classic mistake.

Defining choices and calling people to clear decisive action is a big part of our job as leaders. This needs to be at the forefront in our preaching and our discipling. Satan constantly "muddies the waters" regarding the difference between right and wrong choices. He tempts us to put off the right decisions or gets us to change our minds when the going gets tough. Many awesome disciples have been duped into making bad choices or failing to follow through because they became confused and sentimental.

Making hard decisions can turn around even the most hopeless and desperate situations. In the Old Testament, decision-making was so important that the people were called to come to God for all major decisions. Take into consideration this Scripture:

> *Fashion a breastpiece for making decisions - the work of skilled hands. Make it like the ephod: of gold, and of blue, purple and scarlet yarn, and of finely twisted linen. It is to be square... Then mount four rows of precious stones on it. The first row shall be carnelian, chrysolite and beryl; the second row shall be turquoise, lapis lazuli and emerald; the third row shall be jacinth, agate and amethyst; the fourth row shall be topaz, onyx and jasper. Mount them in gold filigree settings. There are to be twelve stones, one for each of the names of the sons of Israel, each engraved like a seal with the name of one of the twelve tribes.*

Whenever Aaron enters the Holy Place, he will bear the names of the sons of Israel over his heart on the breastpiece of decision as a continuing memorial before the Lord. Also put the Urim and the Thummim in the breastpiece, so they may be over Aaron's heart whenever he enters the presence of the Lord. Thus Aaron will always bear the means of making decisions for the Israelites over his heart before the Lord. (Exodus 28:15-30 Abridged)

Aaron had a special vest called an ephod that he wore to make decisions. Over his chest were stones symbolizing all 12 tribes of Israel. He had to have them on his heart as he went to God for decisions. The ephod itself was made of blue, purple and scarlet yarn, which were the colors of the curtain in the Temple. From Hebrews 10:20, we know that the curtain represents Jesus since it is the way into the Most Holy Place. On the ephod was an Urim and Thummim, to discern what God's will was. When the people brought their radical decisions to God, He showed them the right way to go. By making godly decisions, the people were successful and blessed. We must also have the Kingdom on our hearts. We have the Holy Spirit within us, we have been educated by the Scriptures and we have amazing advisors around us. Therefore, we must make decisive decisions that bring glory to God and success to His family.

Radical decisions have changed the world at so many points in history. However, one of the most poignant was in the early first millennium in Europe during the Middle Ages. This was a time of chaos and brutality, the likes of which have rarely been seen in history. The fall of the Roman Empire had left a vacuum of leadership and authority, which was filled by barbarism. For millions of people, life was short, violent and cruel. It was in the furnace of this chaos that the warriors known as "knights" first emerged. The term "knight" comes from the German word "knecht," meaning servant. In the Middle Ages, as the legends of King Arthur became popular, knights became known as fighters who lived by a code of ethics. They were identified for their respect of authority and defense of the weak. The protection they provided created the haven for many of the kingdoms that emerged at that time. Knights gave their lives to fight against lawlessness and anarchy, and because of their sacrifice, a peaceful civilization could emerge from the fires of Europe.

The McGees lead the mighty IE Region of the CAICC and oversee the Las Vegas International Christian Church.

Without a doubt, the knightly code known as "chivalry" has deep roots in early Christianity and Christian teachings. I believe much of it can be "baptized into Christ" as it has its origins in Scripture. If a generation of leaders were to live by the code of the Scriptures, could they provide the spiritual protection required to allow the church to grow and thrive in this evil age? I believe so with all my heart. Here is the "code of chivalry." I have attached Scriptures to each, which I hope move your heart:

The Code of Chivalry

1. To fear God and maintain His Church. *"And I tell you, you are Peter, and on this rock I will build my church, and the gates of hell shall not prevail against it."* (Matthew 16:18)

2. To serve the liege Lord (leader) in valor and faith. *"...they shouted, 'A sword for the Lord and for Gideon!'"* (Judges 7:20)

3. To protect the weak and defenseless. *"Defend the weak and the fatherless; uphold the cause of the poor and the oppressed."* (Psalm 82:3)

4. To give succor to widows and orphan. *"Religion that is pure and undefiled before God the Father is this: to visit orphans and widows in their affliction, and to keep oneself unstained from the world."* (James 1:2.7)

5. To refrain from the wanton giving of offense. *"But in your hearts revere Christ as Lord. Always be prepared to give an answer to everyone who asks you to give the reason for the hope that you have. But do this with gentleness and respect..."* (1 Peter 3:15)

6. To live by honor and for glory. *"To those who by persistence in doing good seek glory, honor and immortality, He will give eternal life."* (Romans 2:7)

7. To despise pecuniary reward. *"Ill-gotten treasures have no lasting value, but righteousness delivers from death."* (Proverbs 10:2)

8. To fight for the welfare of all. *"The Spirit of the Lord is on me, because He has anointed me to proclaim good news to the poor. He has sent me to proclaim freedom for the prisoners and recovery of sight for the blind, to set the oppressed free..."* (Luke 4:18)

9. To obey those placed in authority. *"Let every person be subject to the governing authorities. For there is no authority except from God, and those that exist have been instituted by God."* (Romans 13:1)

10. To guard the honor of fellow knights. *"Whoever slanders his neighbor secretly I will destroy. Whoever has a haughty look and an arrogant heart I will not endure."* (Psalm 101:5)

11. To eschew unfairness, meanness and deceit. *"Open your mouth, judge righteously, defend the rights of the poor and needy."* (Proverbs 31:9)

12. To keep faith (to be loyal). *"He who pursues righteousness and loyalty finds life, righteousness and honor."* (Proverbs 21:21) *"Many will say they are loyal friends, but who can find one who is truly reliable?"* (Proverbs 20:6)

13. At all times to speak the truth. *"Lying lips are an abomination to the Lord, but those who act faithfully are His delight."* (Proverbs 12:22)

14. To persevere to the end in any enterprise begun. *"Now finish the work, so that your eager willingness to do it may be matched by your completion of it, according to your means."* (2 Corinthians 8:11)

A true knight of the Lord and his fair lady - Coltin and Mandee Rohn - are gallantly leading the SOAR Super Region of LA!

15. To respect the honor of women. *"Likewise, husbands, live with your wives in an understanding way, showing honor to the woman as the weaker vessel, since they are heirs with you of the grace of life, so that your prayers may not be hindered."* (1 Peter 3:7)

16. Never to refuse a challenge from an equal. *"As iron sharpens iron, so one person sharpens another." Proverbs 27:17*

17. Never to turn the back upon a foe. *"But as for the cowardly, the faithless, the detestable, as for murderers, the sexually immoral, sorcerers, idolaters, and all liars, their portion will be in the lake that burns with fire and sulfur, which is the second death?"* (Revelation 21:8)

A few men, the knights who decided to live by this code, changed history forever! The civilization we live in was built on their courage. Be a knight, "knecht," a servant! Be a warrior who lives by a code. Serve your leaders, the authorities that God puts in your life, and do not draw your sword for your own personal reasons but only act under authority. For, *"Fools show their annoyance at once, but the prudent overlook an insult."* (Proverbs 12:16) and

"A person's wisdom yields patience; it is to one's glory to overlook an offense." (Proverbs 19:11) too many people fail to be knights because they act like kings.

Find your king (lower case "k") and be their knight. As Jared McGee once said, "I do not come to our congregational Staff Meeting representing my ministry. I go to my ministry representing my leaders!" What could be done today if a generation of leaders made the decision to become the spiritual knights this burning world so desperately needs?

> *So I tell you this, and insist on it in the Lord, that you must no longer live as the Gentiles do, in the futility of their thinking. They are darkened in their understanding and separated from the life of God because of the ignorance that is in them due to the hardening of their hearts. Having lost all sensitivity, they have given themselves over to sensuality so as to indulge in every kind of impurity, with a continual lust for more.*
>
> *You, however, did not come to know Christ that way. Surely you heard of Him and were taught in Him in accordance with the truth that is in Jesus. You were taught, with regard to your former way of life, to put off your old self, which is being corrupted by its deceitful*

desires; to be made new in the attitude of your minds; and to put on the new self, created to be like God in true righteousness and holiness. (Ephesians 4:17-24)

Dear friends spending some time in the mountains, getting closer to God, one another and making some great ministry and life decisions: Coltin Rohn, Mike Underhill, LuJack Martinez, Blaise Feumba and the author.

What clouds the difference between light and darkness? The answer is sin. Hardened hearts are ignorant and blinded to the right choices. They lose sensitivity and become addicted to sensuality. Sensuality does not necessarily mean sexual sensuality; being addicted to sensuality means becoming addicted to pleasing your senses. People who do this either become desperate thrill-seekers or depressed couch potatoes instead of truth-seekers. Yet, disciples are taught - and must always be reminded - to put off the old way of living, to be responsible and separate from the world.

> "If you are not calling your people to decision, you have made a decision."

What helps us to make great decisions? Biblical principles, godly advice, prayer and fasting. However, God usually makes clear the hard decision that needs to be made. It then becomes more about the courage to take the right action!

I love Coltin Rohn's quote, "If you are not calling your people to decision, you have made a decision." This perfectly captures what this chapter is about!

People become Christians because they want to do great things with their lives. Most want to be called to great decisions and provided accountability so that they can succeed. They want to see incredible miracles happen. If we call our people to great decisions, they will be grateful for it. If they do not see the changes in their lives, they will resent us for never calling them to greatness. Theodore Roosevelt once wrote, "In any moment of decision, the best thing you can do is the right thing, the next best thing is the wrong thing, and the worst thing you can do is nothing."

Noam Chomsky also wrote, "All over the place, from the popular culture to the propaganda system, there is constant pressure to make people feel that they are helpless, that the only role they can have is to ratify decisions and to consume." Making hard decisions is about breaking out of the slavery of the world and taking hold of freedom. But it will take a "catalyst," a true leader, to help make that happen for everyone in your ministry.

Amelia Earhart, the daring woman aviator, once said, "The most difficult thing is the decision to act, the rest is merely tenacity. The fears are paper tigers. You can do anything you decide to do. You can act to change and control your life; and the procedure, the process is its own reward."

Lance and Connie Underhill are a couple who made hard choices for the Lord - leaving riches to become amazing leaders in the Kingdom of God.

Disciples must be given a sense of urgency to act, and that urgency comes from the Scriptures. One of the greatest false doctrines is that we have "plenty of time." The Scriptures are clear. *"For you know quite well that the day of the Lord's return will come unexpectedly, like a thief in the night."* (1 Thessalonians 5:2) It is amazing how excuses melt away in light of Scriptures like this. The knowledge of a sudden return of Christ is one of the greatest motivators for Christians to remain urgent, zealous and committed. It was a topic that was constantly preached in the first-century church.

We might think that defining the difference between God's way and the way of the world - and urging people to obey God's way - is so basic that it is a waste of time to discuss. So why did great leaders like Paul and Moses take it so seriously? Some of their most memorable sayings were about comparing the world's way and God's way.

The famous rabbi Maimonides wrote, "The risk of a wrong decision is preferable to the terror of indecision." On the other hand, "Quick decisions are unsafe decisions," said Sophocles. We must navigate between these extremes every day as a leader in God's Kingdom. There is no gain without danger. While there is no value in reckless, emotional decisions the price of indecision could be even more costly. The more skillful we become at calling people to make decisions, the less unnecessary risk there will be.

While unnecessary risk is not good, making decisions that are risky is an important element of what we do.

> *Ship your grain across the sea;*
> *after many days you may receive a return.*
> *Invest in seven ventures, yes, in eight;*
> *you do not know what disaster may come upon the land.*
> *If clouds are full of water,*
> *they pour rain on the earth.*
> *Whether a tree falls to the south or to the north,*
> *in the place where it falls, there it will lie.*
> *Whoever watches the wind will not plant;*
> *whoever looks at the clouds will not reap.*
> *As you do not know the path of the wind,*
> *or how the body is formed in a mother's womb,*
> *so you cannot understand the work of God,*
> *the Maker of all things.*
> *Sow your seed in the morning,*
> *and at evening let your hands not be idle,*
> *for you do not know which will succeed,*
> *whether this or that,*

or whether both will do equally well. (Ecclesiastes 11:1-6)

The Bible favors risk however it also favors hard work! Do we hire the intern? Do we rent the cheap service location seven miles out of town or the expensive one right next to the top campus? To paraphrase Machiavelli, "do not risk all your treasure without protecting it with all your forces." In other words, take the better location, hire the intern and then share your faith like a maniac with him to make sure your service is full on Sunday!

What if we were to clearly define the differences between the way Satan wants our ministry to think and the way God wants our ministry to think? What if we were to lovingly and carefully define the difference for everyone with whom we are working? What if we called our ministry to definitive changes, to set challenging goals for which we would provide accountability? A minister who can go to the heart of matters and give people clear choices is the minister who will see great things happen in his or her ministry.

Ministry momentum comes from following through on hard decisions. Conversely, a ministry that lacks such a leader cannot distinguish between good choices and bad ones, nor can they exercise their own powers of decision. They will eventually become stagnant and die.

> *But thanks be to God, who always leads us in triumphal procession in Christ and through us spreads everywhere the fragrance of the knowledge of Him. For we are to God the aroma of Christ among those who are being saved and those who are perishing. To the one we are the smell of death; to the other, the fragrance of life.* (2 Corinthians 2:14-16)

When our ministry is defined and advancing by making clear choices, the difference between us and the world will be clear even to those outside the church. To God, we are the aroma of Christ, but to the world, we will become the smell of rot and decay. As spiritual leaders, we are the only ones to help our disciples make excellent and tough spiritual decisions that will propel them to greatness. *"Multitudes, multitudes in the valley of decision! For the day of the Lord is near in the valley of decision."* (Joel 3: 14) Let us define the differences for our ministry. Let us help them to see the true Biblical choices and then call them to powerful, faithful decisions that bring glory to God!

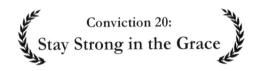

Conviction 20:
Stay Strong in the Grace

The one and only way to true strength: God's grace.

**A true modern-day champion of grace, Prisca Scheidecker
will meet us in Heaven when we pass on to glory.**

Now I commit you to God and to the Word of His grace, which can build you up and give you an inheritance among all those who are sanctified. (Acts 20:32)

What does grace mean? It means overflow, extra and bountiful. God is full of grace and mercy. These qualities He put into all things. He did not make one star; He made billions of stars! He did not make one type of food; He made millions of flavors in incredible abundance! He did not make one kind of flower; He made thousands of species in all the shades of the rainbow! God is graceful in power, in wisdom, in detail, in creation, in glory, in mercy and in all ways!

> *"With grace, nothing stays the same."*

Grace is a bankrupt student finding a winning lottery ticket. Grace is a murderer being forgiven by the family of the victim and given another chance by the courts. Grace is a friend forgiving a betrayal. Grace gives us unlimited chances to change. Grace builds up and gives us an inheritance. With grace, nothing stays the same.

One of my favorite songs simply entitled *Grace* is performed by Bono of U2 and written by Adam Clayton, Dave Evans, Larry Mullen and Paul Hewson.

Grace
She takes the blame
She covers the shame
Removes the stain
It could be her name

Grace
It's a name for a girl
It's also a thought that

Changed the world

And when she walks on the street
You can hear the strings
Grace finds goodness
In everything

Grace
She's got the walk
Not on a ramp or on chalk
She's got the time to talk

She travels outside
Of karma, karma
She travels outside
Of karma

When she goes to work
You can hear the strings
Grace finds beauty
In everything

Grace
She carries a world on her hips
No champagne flute for her lips
No twirls or skips between her fingertips

She carries a pearl
In perfect condition
What once was hurt
What once was friction
What left a mark
No longer stings

Because grace makes beauty
Out of ugly things

Grace finds beauty
In everything

Grace finds goodness in everything

As Bono sang, Grace... changed the world so, Paul wrote to Timothy, *"You then, my son, be strong in the grace that is in Christ Jesus."* (2 Timothy 2:1) Being *"strong in the grace"* starts with the voice in our own heads! If that voice is *"strong in the grace,"* we will be strong indeed! Nevertheless, there are no shortcuts to character and changing how we think. (Romans 12:12) *"For as a man thinketh in his heart, so is he..."* (Proverbs 23:7) *"Strong in the grace"* is about feeling forgiven, feeling grateful, like we have space to breathe with nothing coming at us too fast to handle. Being *"strong in the grace"* means we feel rested, even when we are busy and at peace in "our own skin."

When we are *"strong in the grace"* we are joyful because we trust that God is working through all things, even when there are problems and failures. Remember the words of John F. Kennedy, "Victory has a hundred fathers and defeat is an orphan." When we fail we will often be alone, while others run for the hills, but if we are *"strong in the grace"* we will own the failure and learn from our mistakes. When we are *"strong in the grace"* we consider trouble *"pure joy,"* because we know that it is making us *"mature"* (James 1:2-8), and that *"God will give [us] a way out."* (1 Corinthians 10:13)

When we are *"strong in the grace,"* we have that elusive "life force" that ministers need to have. In John 18:1-6 we see Jesus' force of character, even under duress.

271

When he had finished praying, Jesus left with his disciples and crossed the Kidron Valley. On the other side there was a garden, and he and his disciples went into it.

Now Judas, who betrayed him, knew the place, because Jesus had often met there with his disciples. So Judas came to the garden, guiding a detachment of soldiers and some officials from the chief priests and the Pharisees. They were carrying torches, lanterns and weapons.

Jesus, knowing all that was going to happen to him, went out and asked them, "Who is it you want?"

"Jesus of Nazareth," they replied.

"I am he," Jesus said. (And Judas the traitor was standing there with them.) When Jesus said, "I am he," they drew back and fell to the ground.

Jesus is at one of the most difficult moments in his life and yet an armed group falls at His feet at the mere sight of Him! Life force is character, being completely clean of sin, having closeness to God; it is about letting people feel the full weight of who we are.

Those who are *"strong in the grace"* are humble; they seek advice; and they ask godly people for help after asking God for help so they do not get overwhelmed. They do not drag others down. (Philippians 4:4-7) They use the Bible to do all the heavy lifting they need to do. They are disciplined in their thinking: demolishing arguments, capturing every impure and discouraging thought, and making it obedient to Christ. (2 Corinthians 10:5) Disciples who are *"strong in the grace"* take time for solid quiet times, romantic times with their wives or husbands, they "catch themselves" by taking time away with God and those closest to them, so they never become haggard and exhausted. (Mark 1:35) Even when they talk to themselves in the comfort of their own heads, they are gracious and think in terms of God's Word.

One powerful example of being *"strong in the grace"* must be my dear sister and friend, Prisca Scheidecker. She was a sister with abounding grace. She made every day better by her joyful presence. Her love for her incredible husband Philippe and her children Rebecca and Theo was ever present. She forgave easily, believed in people at a glance, and always thought the best of people. When she went on to glory on December 22, 2016, she left a massive hole in the hearts of so many. The week she died of breast cancer, she had led Women's Midweek Service in Paris, France, and studied the Bible with a young convert. She died happy and full of faith. I wish every disciple could go to glory like Prisca. I cannot wait to be with her in glory!

What saddens me is seeing disciples who are not like Prisca and have not yet learning to be *"strong in the grace."* The worries of life, the stresses of change, the guilt of sin, the sickness of heart from unfulfilled dreams - as well as the anger and bitterness from a lack of forgiveness - make them lifeless and washed out. (Matthew 6:23) They block a close relationship with God. While other disciples are flourishing, they are dying because of their dependence on their talent, intellect and sentimental relationships. Their independence from God will not let them take advantage of His grace.

Today on campuses, suicide is the second greatest cause of death after automobile accidents. Why? Young people - put in the graceless world where grades are gods and left alone to sink or swim - often respond with hopelessness and despair. Grace is the ointment that will make campus students strong for the battle. Countless thousands who do not have grace sadly choose to take their own lives instead.

The Scripture, 1 Peter 1:3 states, *"Praise be to the God and Father of our Lord Jesus Christ! In His great mercy He has given us new birth into a living hope through the resurrection of Jesus Christ from the dead..."* At the end of the day, what does it mean to be *"strong in the grace?"* It means that as disciples, we have a new and living hope in the resurrection. It does not mean that we will not have to persevere through terrible trouble and even death. It means we will do it with a grin (a small grin at times), because we believe that we will participate in the resurrection of the dead. That is the secret to being *"strong in the grace."*

Mike and Brittany Underhill dynamically lead the City of Angels International Christian Church Campus Ministry!

It means that even on the most terrible of days, we have a vision in our minds of the glorious day of the Lord. *"Strong in the grace"* means feeling and knowing we are forgiven every day, but especially on that day. There is no other way to be truly strong in this life. This is not just about feeling better; it is about spiritual survival. If Satan can get you discouraged, after a failure, a loss or an unexpected change, then he has the initiative. In the words of the famous sword fighter and Samurai Miyamoto Musashi, "To renew applies when we are fighting with the enemy, and... there is no possible resolution. We must abandon our efforts, think of the situation in a fresh spirit then win. To renew, when we are deadlocked with the enemy, means that without changing our circumstance we change our spirit and win through a different technique." Someone who has mastered this will be undefeatable.

The age-old question of course is, "Is grace a license to sin or to take sin lightly?" Paul replies in Romans 6:1-2, *"What shall we say, then? Shall we go on sinning so that grace may increase? By no means! We died to sin; how can we live in it any longer?"* Someone who desperately wants to be forgiven of their sin does not want to get straight back into it.

In his letter to Titus, Paul writes:

> *For the grace of God has appeared that offers salvation to all people. It teaches us to say "No" to ungodliness and worldly passions, and to live self-controlled, upright and godly lives in this present age, while we wait for the blessed hope - the appearing of the glory of our great God and Savior, Jesus Christ, who gave Himself for us to redeem us from all wickedness and to purify for Himself a people that are His very own, eager to do what is good.* (Titus 2:11-14)

Disciples who are *"strong in the grace"* have been taught to say *"no"* to sin. They live upright and respectable lives and are eager to do what is good, knowing sincerely that they belong to Christ. They are not just men and women for God - they are men and women of God!

Conversely, Jonah warns us strongly, *"Those who cling to worthless idols forfeit the grace that could be theirs."* (Jonah 2:8) Nothing in life should give us more comfort than the grace of Christ. Proverbs 28:13 puts it this way, *"He who conceals his sins does not prosper, but whoever confesses and renounces them finds mercy."* If we hide in the darkness, we appear to be free of sin. However, someone who is truly in the light is open, and other people can see their imperfections and shortcomings. God's love fills in the gaps we leave and helps us to avoid sin in the first place! *"Through love and faithfulness sin is atoned for; through the fear of the Lord evil is avoided."* (Proverbs 16:6)

In 1 Corinthians 15:10, Paul writes, *"But by the grace of God I am what I am, and His grace to me was not without effect. No, I worked harder than all of them - yet not I, but the grace of God that was with me."* People who are "strong in the grace" are hard workers! They have a godly ambition to do good for the Kingdom. Put them in any situation and they are a force of nature, changing their environment for the better!

Right now, are we *"strong in the grace"* or is our strength present only when things are going our way? What about those we are discipling? Can we help them to build convictions about being *"strong in the grace?"* Can we unleash the "life force" that comes from feeling adored by God? God and His church are desperate for people who will be *"strong in the grace."*

Get strong in the only way that really counts - get *"strong in the grace"* that is in Christ Jesus.

Epilogue

In the past twenty days, we have taken a journey through many different facets of ministry. Some of them may have been very familiar, others may have served as a good reminder, and perhaps others were a completely new way of looking at the ministry. It is my sincere prayer that this book has inspired you in your ministry work. As Joseph Campbell, one of the founders of the Restoration Movement, once said, "God has left the evangelization of the world up to the church..." This a great point for any sermon. As we advance with this task in mind, we all get into tough situations and need solid Biblical advice on how to get out of a bind, move forward and try in new ways that we had not considered before. I hope you have a few of those now under your belt.

I am sure it is obvious to many who know me that my primary audience in writing this book is you, my two sons, Junior and David. I pray you become leaders and that the Scriptures and your father's advice comfort you in times of hardship. I love you both very much. Similar to some of my favorite books of my youth Hizens *Hagakure*, Julius Caesar's *de Bello Gallico*, Che's *On Guerrilla Warfare*, Machiavelli's *The Prince*, Miyamoto Musashi's *The Book of Five Rings* or Marcus Aurelius' *Meditations*, this is a family book of Biblical ministry lessons. I do not presume to put myself in the same intellectual league as these thinkers. However, to protect our spiritual family from Satan's schemes we must strive to be. I hope this book not only comforts and encourages you but countless other leaders as you struggle with the realities of being a ministry practitioner.

Come what may, be it unity or rebellion, growth or pruning, good times or bad, my prayer is that your heart is to put the Scriptures into practice.

As we read at the beginning, the number twenty, or half of forty, is the number of qualification, competence or beginning. Like Jacob and Joseph, like all able-bodied men over the age of twenty who served in Israel's army or who were held accountable for their sins in the desert, like the Levites, twenty years old, who began to serve in the Temple, this book has twenty chapters. It represents the beginning, responsibility and learning. This book has twenty chapters because this represents the beginning of the road to understanding visionary leadership principles of ministry - not the end. Enjoy the journey, but take it seriously. You do not want your life to merely serve as a road sign or warning for others - you want it to take you home.

It is now time to act! Though you will stumble and fall many times, if you stay close to God, you will always rise again. ***"For though the righteous fall seven times, they rise again, but the wicked stumble when calamity strikes."*** (Proverbs 24:16) Be a minister! Be God's ambassador! Serve the leaders that God has put in your life as a knight! Go forward into the world and change it!

From the bottom of my heart - God bless you!

Tim Kernan
July 4, 2017

Contact the Author:

facebook.com/tim.kernan
twitter.com/timkernan
tim@usd21.org

Made in the USA
San Bernardino, CA
16 July 2017